Contents

About This Book

*M*em Fox is Australia's most celebrated children's author. Her best-selling books have enchanted readers Down Under for more than 20 years. But the author's work has a universal appeal that charms readers from all parts of the world. Her imaginative stories are told in a lyrical, poetic language sure to touch the hearts of children everywhere. Whether writing about the tender relationship between a young boy and his 96-year-old friend (*Wilfrid Gordon McDonald Partridge*) or a lonely little koala who decides to compete in the Olympics (*Koala Lou*), Fox has a knack for exploring the feelings and experiences of childhood through lovable characters readers instantly relate to. From an accident-prone little girl (*Harriet, You'll Drive Me Wild!*) to a patient mama bear (*Sleepy Bears*), Mem Fox's characters tell the kinds of stories that everyone can recognize. But these stories do more than capture the real-life experiences of children; they also capture their soaring imaginations. There is an element of fantasy in many of Fox's books (*Possum Magic, The Magic Hat*) that opens the door to a magical world where anything can happen. And perhaps the most magical thing of all is the love of reading that her work has inspired in children all over the world.

The activities in this book are designed to help you get the most out of Mem Fox's literature in your classroom. You'll find detailed discussion guides to use before and after reading each book, plus cross-curricular activities to extend children's learning in a variety of subject areas, including language arts, social studies, math, science, movement, and art. On pages 6–8, you'll find general activities to enhance your study of the author's work. On the pages that follow, you'll find activities to use with all 12 featured Mem Fox titles. Each book unit includes:

◎ **About the Book:** Story description and synopsis.

◎ **Concepts and Themes:** Central themes and concepts included in the story.

◎ **Before and After Reading:** Discussion tips for enhancing children's literature experiences by building background knowledge and predicting, retelling, and relating the story to their own lives.

◎ **Extension Activities:** Activity ideas for reinforcing and expanding children's learning across the curriculum.

◎ **Word Play:** Mini-lessons for focusing on a specific literacy element in the text.

On the last page of this book, you'll find culminating activities for a Mem Fox celebration. You can use these ideas to wrap up your study of the author's work and celebrate all that children have learned. Whether you choose to do an in-depth author study or simply dip into her books from time to time throughout the year, this book will provide you with everything you need to bring Mem Fox's special brand of reading magic to life in your classroom. So open a Mem Fox book and let the enchantment begin!

■SCHOLASTIC

Teaching With Favorite
Mem Fox
Books

BY **PAMELA CHANKO**

NEW YORK • TORONTO • LONDON • AUCKLAND • SYDNEY
MEXICO CITY • NEW DELHI • HONG KONG • BUENOS AIRES

Teaching *Resources*

For Nora and Nicholas,
students of the world,
whose journey upon it
is only beginning.

ACKNOWLEDGMENTS

*Special thanks to Kama Einhorn for her generous support, her unfailing good humor,
and her belief in possum magic.*

Jacket illustrations from *Wilfred Gordon McDonald Partridge* reprinted by permission of Kane/Miller Book Publishers.

Jacket illustrations from *Koala Lou* and *Whoever You Are* used with permission of Harcourt, Inc. All rights reserved.

Cover and interior design by Kathy Massaro
Interior art by James Graham Hale

ISBN: 0-439-63521-7
Copyright © 2005 by Pamela Chanko.
All rights reserved.
Printed in the U.S.A.

1 2 3 4 5 6 7 8 9 10   40   13 12 11 10 09 08 07 06 05

About Mem Fox

Mem Fox was born in Melbourne, Australia, on March 5, 1946. Her full name is Merrion Frances, but she has been called "Mem" ever since she can remember. At the age of 6 months, Mem moved to Africa with her parents, who were missionaries. She grew up on the Hope Fountain Mission, a few miles from the city of Bulawayo in Zimbabwe. At the mission school, Mem learned to write outdoors under a tree by drawing letters of the alphabet in the earth with her fingers. Later, her class graduated to writing on slates, which she says "squeaked horribly." Now, the author writes the first drafts of her celebrated books on yellow paper with a 4B pencil before moving to a computer.

In the mid-1960s, Mem left Africa and traveled to England to go to drama school. In 1969, she married her husband, Malcolm, a teacher, and in 1970 they moved to Adelaide, South Australia, where they have lived ever since. They have one daughter, Chloë, born in 1971.

In her early 30s, Mem went to university. Her daughter loved to read, so Mem decided to take a course in children's literature: a choice that would change her life. It was during this course that she wrote *Hush the Invisible Mouse*, which later became *Possum Magic*. The book was rejected nine times over five years, but eventually went on to become the best-selling children's book ever in Australia. Since its publication in 1983, Mem has gone on to write more than 25 picture books for children.

However, Mem admits that writing is her "second love"—her first is teaching. Her training in literacy led her to what she says is "the great passion" of her life: studying ways to help children learn to read. She taught as an associate professor of literacy studies at the School of Education at Flinders University, South Australia, for 24 years. She retired from full-time teaching in 1996, but is still an esteemed literacy consultant in many countries around the world. She has also published books on children's literacy for adults, including *Reading Magic* (Harcourt, 2001) and *Radical Reflections: Passionate Opinions on Teaching, Learning, and Living* (Harcourt, 1993). Her work as an author and teacher has led to numerous awards, including the 1990 Dromkeen medal for distinguished services to children's literature, the 2001 South Australian "SA Great" award for literature, and the Australian Prime Minister's Centenary medal in 2003.

Fox continues to write books for both adults and children from her home in Adelaide. Although the author admits that writing picture books is very hard work, she also finds it extremely rewarding. "Writing them well means writing and rewriting," Mem says of her children's stories. "I do it because I love it when kids say, 'I love your books!'"

Exploring the Books of Mem Fox: Activities for Any Time

In addition to the activities suggested for each featured title, try the following ideas to build on children's literacy learning, make connections between stories, and enhance their understanding of the author and her work as a whole.

Hop to Your Favorite Story

You can add a whimsical Australian touch to a class graph with the kangaroo marker below. Try this ongoing graphing activity as you read Mem Fox's books.

◎ Each time children finish a story, write the title on a large index card and post it on the left side of the board. Once you have read two Mem Fox books, you can begin graphing.

◎ Provide each child with a copy of the kangaroo graph marker and invite children to label it with their name. Place a bit of removable adhesive on the back of each kangaroo. Then have children attach their kangaroo to the graph next to the story they liked best.

◎ Continue to add titles to your graph as you read new books. Each time you add a new title, invite children to reevaluate their choice. If their favorite story has changed, they can hop their kangaroo to the row of their new favorite. Discuss the results of your graph on a regular basis and invite children to share what they enjoyed about their current favorite story.

**kangaroo
graph
marker
pattern**

Character Venns

Help children explore the characters in Fox's stories with a Venn diagram.

1. Draw two overlapping circles on a sheet of chart paper and label each with the name of a character. Choose fairly comparable characters from different stories, such as Miss Nancy from *Wilfrid Gordon McDonald Partridge* and Lily Laceby from *Night Noises*, or Hush from *Possum Magic* and Koala Lou from *Koala Lou.*

2. Invite children to describe each character and his or her actions in the story as you write their ideas on the diagram. Character facts that apply to only one character should be placed in that circle; facts that apply to both characters should be placed in the intersection.

3. When your diagram is full, invite children to look at their facts and explain how the two characters are alike and different. Which character would they most like to meet, and why?

Connections to the Language Arts Standards

The activities in this book are designed to support you in meeting the following standards outlined by the Mid-continent Research for Education and Learning (MCREL), an organization that collects and synthesizes national and state K–12 curriculum standards.

Uses the general skills and strategies of the reading process:

◆ Uses mental images based on pictures and print to aid in comprehension of text

◆ Uses meaning clues (for example, picture captions, title, cover, headings, story structure, story topic) to aid comprehension and make predictions about content (for example, action, events, character's behavior)

Uses the general skills and strategies of the writing process:

◆ Uses strategies to organize written work (for example, includes a beginning, middle, and ending; uses a sequence of events)

◆ Uses writing and other methods (for example, using letters or phonetically spelled words, telling, dictating, making lists) to describe familiar persons, places, objects, or experiences

◆ Writes in a variety of forms or genres (for example, picture books, friendly letters, stories, poems, information pieces, invitations, personal experience narratives, messages, responses to literature)

◆ Writes for different purposes (for example, to entertain, inform, learn, communicate ideas)

Uses listening and speaking strategies for different purposes:

◆ Makes contributions in class and group discussions (for example, reports on ideas and personal knowledge about a topic, initiates conversations, connects ideas and experiences with those of others)

◆ Asks and responds to questions (for example, about the meaning of a story, about the meaning of words or ideas)

◆ Follows rules of conversation and group discussion (for example, takes turns, raises hand to speak, stays on topic, focuses attention on speaker)

◆ Gives and responds to oral directions

◆ Recites and responds to familiar stories, poems, and rhymes with patterns (for example, relates information to own life; describes character, setting, plot)

Source: *Content Knowledge: A Compendium of Standards and Benchmarks for K–12 Education* (4th ed.). Mid-continent Research for Education and Learning, 2004.

Adventures in Australia

Mem Fox is a native of Australia, and her heritage has influenced her writing, particularly in such stories as *Koala Lou* and *Possum Magic*. As you explore Fox's work, you might like to do a mini-unit on her homeland as well. Australia is a fascinating place, full of exotic animals and beautiful, varied landscapes. You'll find several activities in this book to help you explore Australia's wildlife, customs, and culture (see the units for *Koala Lou* and *Possum Magic*, plus Culminating Activities on the last page). Try these books to help children learn even more about the land Down Under.

◎ *Colors of Australia* by Lynn Ainsworth Olawsky (Carolrhoda, 1997). From the cream-colored sheep to the green eucalyptus trees, this book explores all of the beautiful colors that make up Australia.

◎ *Look What Came From Australia* by Kevin Davis (Orchard, 2000). This informative book describes many things that originated in Australia, including inventions, sports and games, food, and musical instruments.

◎ *One Woolly Wombat* by Rod Trinca (Kane Miller, 1985). This Aussie counting book features rhyming descriptions of 14 different animals, from wombats to koalas to magpies to platypuses!

◎ *Postcards From Australia* by Helen Arnold (Steck-Vaughn, 1996). This book features a collection of postcards written as if by children traveling Down Under. Beautiful photographs take children on a tour of Australia's outback, cities, beaches, and deserts.

◎ *A Visit to Australia* by Rachel Bell (Heinemann, 1999). Photographs and simple text explore Australia's landmarks, food, transportation, and culture.

Wilfrid Gordon McDonald Partridge

❖

(KANE/MILLER, 1984)

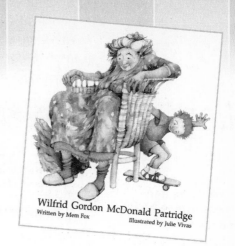

Wilfrid Gordon McDonald Partridge
Written by Mem Fox · Illustrated by Julie Vivas

Wilfrid Gordon McDonald Partridge loves all his neighbors at the old people's home next door, but his favorite is 96-year-old Miss Nancy. When Wilfrid hears that Miss Nancy has lost her memory, he decides to find out just what a memory is, so he can help her get it back. This beautiful story celebrates the special relationship that can be shared between the very young and the very old.

Before Reading

Invite children to share any special experiences they have had with people much older than they are. Do children have grandparents or a favorite older neighbor or family friend? What makes this person special to them? Ask:

❋ What kinds of activities do you do with your grandparent or older friend? What sorts of things do you talk about together?

❋ Has this person ever taught you anything special, such as how to make a favorite recipe or practice a certain skill?

❋ How is spending time with an older friend different from spending time with someone your own age? How is it similar?

After Reading

First, help children understand the concept of memory. Ask:

❋ What does it mean to *remember* something? Do you remember what you ate for breakfast this morning? How about what you did after school yesterday?

❋ Can you remember anything special you did a long time ago, such as going on a trip or outing with your family? What do you remember about it?

Next, explain that a *memory* is anything that a person remembers from the past: It can be something that happened a short time ago or a long time ago. Discuss how Wilfrid helped Miss Nancy remember important events in her life by bringing her special objects. Ask:

❋ Have you ever brought back a souvenir from a trip to help you remember it?

❋ Do you have any items from when you were younger, such as a favorite blanket or stuffed animal? What things do these items help you remember?

Then invite children to talk about Wilfrid's relationship with Miss Nancy. Ask:

❋ How did Wilfrid show kindness toward Miss Nancy? How did he help her?

❋ What were some things that Wilfrid and Miss Nancy had in common?

Concepts and Themes

▲▲▲▲▲▲

✺ time and memory

✺ intergenerational friendship

✺ giving

Word Play

Look through the book with children to find the five descriptive definitions for memory: *something warm, something from long ago, something that makes you cry, something that makes you laugh,* and *something as precious as gold.* Then invite children to come up with their own definitions for memory.

Write the following stem on a sentence strip: "A memory is something _____." Encourage children to suggest descriptive words or phrases to complete the sentence, such as *special* or *that makes you smile.* Have children write or dictate their sentence endings on additional strips. They can take turns putting the strips together and reading the completed sentences aloud. (For an art extension, see *Gifts for Miss Nancy,* right.)

Gifts for Miss Nancy (Art and Language Arts)

In the story, Wilfrid asks each of his neighbors to answer the question "What's a memory?" He gets a variety of definitions: something warm, something from long ago, something happy, something sad, something that makes you cry and something "as precious as gold." To help Miss Nancy, Wilfrid finds an object that he thinks fits each of these descriptions. Invite children to make their own interpretations by creating collages showing the gifts they would give to Miss Nancy.

1. Write the five descriptions of memory on the board or a sheet of chart paper. Then invite children to look through old magazines and cut out pictures of things that fit each description. Encourage them to use their imaginations. For instance, "something warm" could be a blanket or a cup of soup, but it could also be a loving hug or a playful puppy. If children have a special idea for a gift, they can also draw their own pictures. Help children label their collages to show which definition each picture represents.

2. When children's collages are complete, post them on a bulletin board for display and discussion. Invite children to share why they chose each item and tell how it fits that particular description of memory.

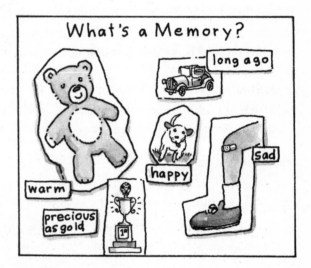

Make New Friends (Social Skills and Art)

Show children the value of love, care, and respect for older generations by making a visit to a retirement home or senior community. Children might prepare a performance for their visit, such as a sing-along or a short play. If a visit is not possible, invite children to send special gifts to the residents. For instance, they might create pictures or posters to brighten the walls of the home, send a bouquet of "flowers" made from chenille sticks and colored tissue, or even create a mural on craft paper of a sunny outdoor scene. Whatever your contribution, it is sure to be a welcome surprise that will brighten each resident's day.

Class Time Capsule (Social Studies)

A major theme in the story is that special objects can bring back special memories. You can reinforce this concept by creating a class time capsule.

1. Explain to children that a time capsule is a collection of objects that help people remember a certain period of time. Tell them that they will be creating a time capsule to remember their year at school.

2. Invite children to decorate a large shoebox with collage materials such as tissue paper and ribbon. Create a label for the box reading "Our Class Time Capsule."

3. Next, invite children to suggest items to place in the box. If someone were to find the box years later, what items would help this person see what the classroom was like and what kinds of activities children did?

4. Invite children to continue adding items to the time capsule throughout the year. Encourage them to explain the significance of each item they suggest. At the end of the year, open the box and share the memories! Invite children to recall the circumstances behind each "artifact" and explain what made them special.

Clothespin Time Lines (Math and Social Studies)

Help children learn about memories and the passage of time as you reinforce sequencing skills with this time line activity.

1. Work with children to brainstorm a list of important events in their lives. These might include accomplishments (such as learning to tie their shoes) and any big changes that have taken place for them (such as moving to a new town).

2. Provide children with several sheets of drawing paper and invite them to illustrate one event on each sheet. Help them write or dictate captions for their pictures as well. Encourage children to include how old they were at the time of each event, if possible.

3. Hang one string of yarn in the classroom for each child (across a wall or from the ceiling, if it is low enough). Attach several clothespins to each string.

4. Invite children to hang their pictures from the clothespins in sequential order to create a time line.

Additional Resources

Can You Do This, Old Badger?
by Eve Bunting
(Harcourt, 2000)

Follow Little Badger and Old Badger on a delightful afternoon walk as they discover all the things they can learn from each other.

The Chicken Salad Club
by Marsha Diane Arnold
(Dial, 1998)

When Nathaniel's 100-year-old "Greatpaw" shares stories of the "old days," the children of the neighborhood begin to see its older residents in a whole new way.

Miss Opal's Auction
by Susan Vizurraga
(Henry Holt, 2000)

This story celebrates the passing on of memories from one generation to the next as Miss Opal gives young Annie a cookbook full of precious traditions.

When I Am Old With You
by Angela Johnson
(Orchard, 1990)

In this poignant story, children see that loved ones do not have to be the same age to make wonderful memories together.

Oral Histories (Language Arts and Social Studies)

Help children make a connection with members of the older generation as they learn about long-ago times by inviting a grandparent or an older neighbor to visit the classroom for an interview. (Children might also like to interview older friends and relatives at home.) Prepare for the interview by brainstorming a list of questions children would like to ask. Interesting topics might include:

◎ Where did you live as a child? What was your neighborhood like?

◎ How did people dress when you were young? What did you wear to school each day?

◎ What was your favorite game or toy?

◎ What is your most special childhood memory?

You might ask your visitor to bring in childhood photographs of him- or herself, as well as pictures of family and friends. Tape-record the interviews if possible, and place the cassettes in the listening center. These are the kinds of stories children will want to hear told again and again.

Make a Memory Basket (Language Arts and Art)

Wilfrid Gordon brought a basket full of memories to Miss Nancy. Invite children to use the reproducible on page 13 to create their own memory baskets.

1. Make one copy of page 13 for each child. Help children cut along the dotted lines to separate the two parts of the activity sheet. To create the basket, have children cut along the line to make a slit. Then have children glue the basket to a separate sheet of construction paper. (They should only glue it around the edges.) Be sure they do not glue down the open slit—this will create the "memory pocket." Invite children to decorate the basket and label it with their name.

2. Next, help children complete the memory sheet. Encourage them to think of a special memory and draw a picture to illustrate the event. The memory might be anything from an exciting trip to a quiet afternoon with a loved one. Help children write or dictate a caption describing their memory.

3. Have children place their memory sheet in the basket pocket. Display the baskets on a wall of the classroom for children to share and enjoy.

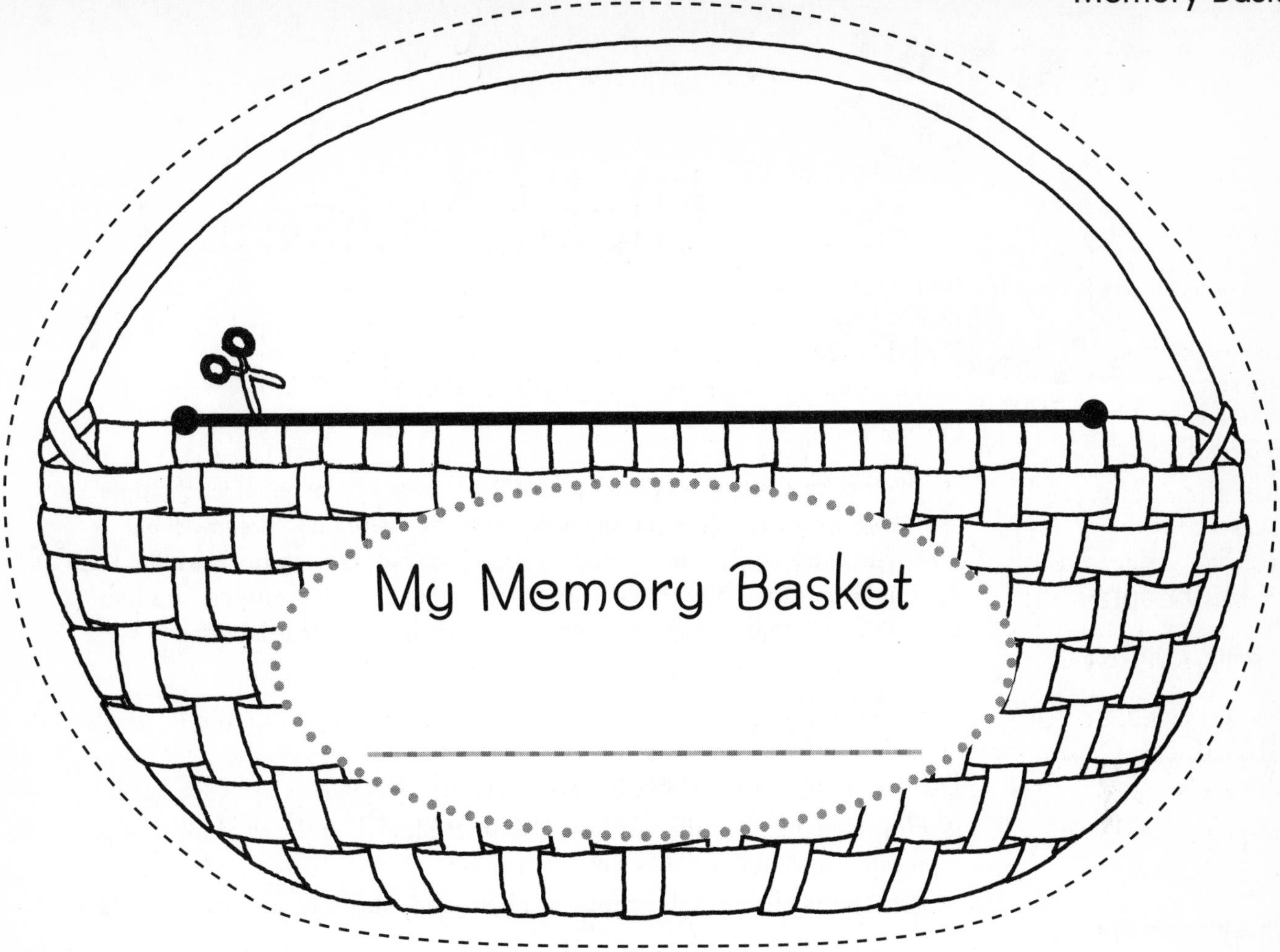

My Memory Basket

_____

My Favorite Memory

○
○
○
○
○
○
○

WRITTEN BY Mem Fox ILLUSTRATED BY Terry Denton

Night Noises

❖

(HARCOURT, 1989)

Concepts and Themes

▲ ▲ ▲ ▲ ▲ ▲

- ☼ noises and sounds, hearing

- ☼ birthday celebrations

- ☼ nighttime, sleep, dreams

Lily Laceby is nearly 90 years old and lives alone with her dog, Butch Aggie. One stormy winter's night, Lily falls asleep by the fire and dreams of old times. But Butch Aggie is awakened by strange sounds coming from outside. Who could it be on such a night? The noisy suspense builds until... Surprise! It's time for Lily's ninetieth birthday party, and everyone has come to celebrate!

Before Reading

Begin a discussion with children about nighttime. Ask:

* How is nighttime different from daytime? How does the sky look at night compared to how it looks during the day?
* What sorts of things do you do at night that you don't do during the day?

Next, show children the cover of the book and read the title aloud. Ask:

* What kinds of noises can you hear at night? When you are in bed at night, what sounds can you hear from outside? How do they make you feel?
* What kinds of noises do you think the lady and her dog will hear in the story? What do you think will happen?

After Reading

Encourage children to retell parts of the story and share their reactions by asking:

* What kinds of noises woke up Butch Aggie? Why do you think he started to growl?
* As I read the story, what did you think the noises were? If you heard noises like that at night, how would it make you feel?
* What did the noises turn out to be? Did the ending of the story surprise you? Why or why not?

Next, discuss Lily Laceby and help children connect to her experiences. Ask:

* What do you think Lily Laceby was dreaming about? Who was the young girl in the pictures? What kinds of things do you dream about at night?
* Do you think Lily was scared when the noises finally woke her up? Why? How do you think she felt when she opened the door?
* Do you think Lily enjoyed her birthday party? How would you feel if your family and friends threw you a surprise party?

Name That Noise! (Science)

Invite children to explore their sense of hearing and test their listening skills with a game show–style guessing game.

1. In advance, write several simple noise-making instructions on small slips of paper. Examples might include: *clap your hands; snap your fingers; clap two erasers together; tap a pencil on a table; crumple a piece of paper; stomp your foot;* and so on. Place the slips in a paper bag.

2. Next, choose three children to be the "contestants." Have them stand at the front of the room and give them bandannas or strips of cloth to cover their eyes. Then pass the paper bag to a volunteer in the "audience" and let him or her silently pick an instruction and then make the noise one or more times. Have the contestants raise their hand when they think they can identify the noise correctly. The first child to raise his or her hand makes the first guess. If the guess is incorrect, the other contestants can make guesses. (If you like, you can keep score by giving one point for each correct guess.)

3. Continue to pass the bag around the room, letting different volunteers choose and make the noises. When the bag is empty, discuss the results. How many noises were the contestants able to identify? Write new noises, choose new contestants, and play again!

Day Noises, Night Noises (Social Studies, Science, and Art)

Lily Laceby is surprised by the noises she hears during a quiet evening at home. What kinds of noises can children hear in their own homes? How do they change from daytime to nighttime? Use this take-home activity to find out.

1. Invite children to draw a simple map of their home. The maps do not need to be completely accurate, but children should make sure they show every room. Gather children's maps and make a photocopy so that each child has two. Have them label one map "Day Noises" and the other "Night Noises."

2. Let children take their maps home and ask family members to help them fill in sounds on each map. Children can take a walk around their homes during the day and at night, writing down the sounds they hear in each room. For instance, children might hear bacon sizzling in the kitchen in the morning, and the sound of a dishwasher gurgling at night.

3. Have children bring in their maps to share with the class. How are the sounds in children's homes alike and different? What noises are more likely to be heard during the day and at night?

Word Play

Night Noises provides a perfect opportunity to teach onomatopoeia—words that imitate sounds. Look through the book with children for the sound words that appear in large, graphic type. Words they might find include: *click, clack, crunch, bang, creak,* and *crack.* Write the words on chart paper and invite children to suggest additional examples of onomatopoeia to expand the list, such as *buzz, whoosh,* and *squeak.* Children can use the words to write their own noisy story!

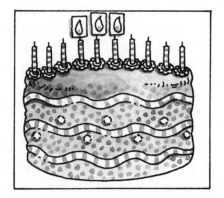

▲▲▲▲▲▲▲▲▲▲▲

Additional
Resources

Nana's Birthday Party
by Amy Hest
(William Morrow, 1993)

As two girls help their
grandmother prepare for her
annual birthday party, they
hear about her special
memories and help create
new ones.

The Napping House
by Audrey Wood
(Harcourt, 1984)

Children will delight in this
cumulative tale of a dozing
granny who is joined in her
nap by one creature after
another…including one tiny,
wakeful flea. Everybody up!

The Very Noisy Night
by Diana Hendry
(Dutton, 1999)

It's late at night, and lots of
scary noises are keeping Little
Mouse awake—but Big Mouse
has a comforting explanation
for each and every one.

What's That Noise?
by William Carman
(Random House, 2002)

In this tale of noises in the
night, a young boy is
awakened by a spooky sound
and bravely sets out to find
the source—Dad's snoring!

Birthday Blowout Story Mat (Math)

At the end of the story, Lily Laceby's family surprises her with a wonderful party and a cake full of candles. Since Lily is 90, there are plenty of candles to blow out on her cake! Use the story mat on page 17 to help children practice math skills as they "blow out" candles on their own birthday cake.

1. Make a copy of the story mat for each child and invite children to decorate their cakes with crayons, markers, and glitter. Then have children cut out the candle flames and place one on top of each candle.

2. Recite the following poem as children act it out on their mats. Have them remove a flame piece each time they "blow out" a candle.

> Ten candles light up the birthday cake,
> So take a deep breath, for goodness' sake!
> Now blow one out and dance about,
> How many candles left to blow out?

3. Have children count the candles that are still "lit" on their cakes to find the answer. Then recite the poem again, starting with the number nine. Continue until only one flame is left, and end with this verse:

> One candle lights up the birthday cake,
> So take a deep breath, for goodness' sake!
> Now blow it out and dance about,
> No more candles left to blow out!

4. For a greater challenge, give children a different number of candles to blow out on each verse. You can even incorporate number sentences, for instance:

> Now blow 2 + 1 out…

and so on.

Birthday Blowout Story Mat

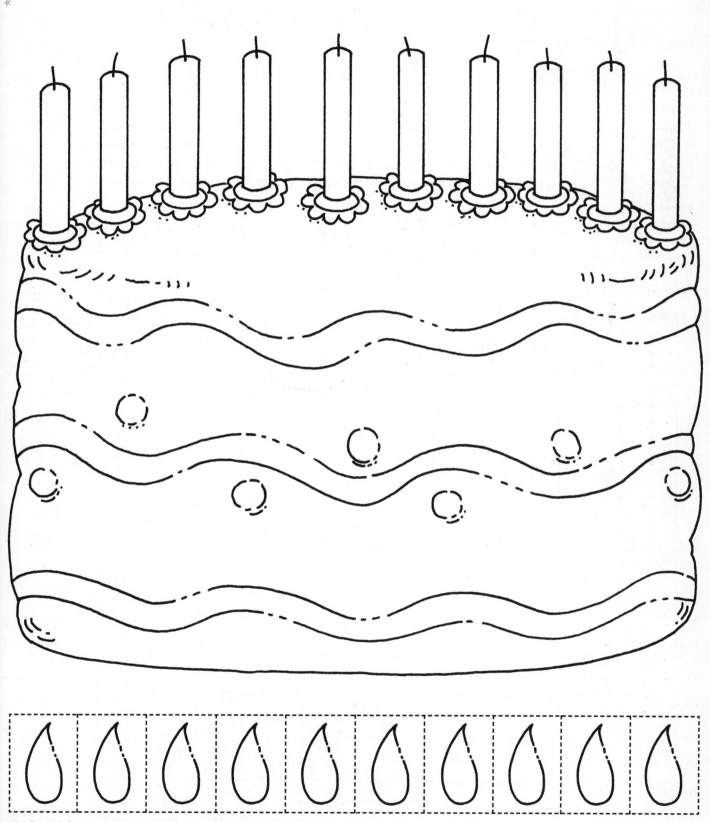

Teaching With Favorite Mem Fox Books   Scholastic Teaching Resources

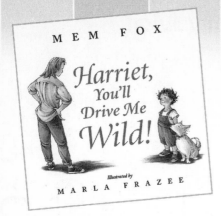

M E M F O X

Harriet,
You'll
Drive Me
Wild!

Illustrated by
M A R L A F R A Z E E

Harriet, You'll Drive Me Wild!

(H A R C O U R T, 2 0 0 0)

Harriet Harris doesn't mean to cause trouble. Sometimes it just happens. And Harriet's mother doesn't mean to lose her temper. But after a long day of mishaps and messes, she just does. This delightful, realistic story shows that parents and children can make mistakes—and still love one another after all.

Concepts and Themes

▲▲▲▲▲▲

✸ feelings

✸ parents

✸ making mistakes

Before Reading

Introduce the story by beginning a discussion about making mistakes. Encourage children to share their feelings by asking:

✳ Have you ever made a mistake? Have you ever done something and wished later that you hadn't done it, such as spilling a glass of milk or making a big mess? What happened? How did it make you feel?

✳ What can you do after you make a mistake? Have you ever apologized or said "I'm sorry" after doing something you wished you hadn't? Did it make you feel better? How?

Show children the cover of the book. Ask:

✳ How do you think the little girl in this picture is feeling? How might her mother be feeling? What can you tell about the story from the title?

After Reading

After reading, take a picture walk back through the story and use the illustrations to talk about the characters' feelings. Ask questions such as:

✳ How does Harriet's mother feel in each part of the story? How does her face change with each mistake Harriet makes?

✳ How does Harriet feel after the pillow rips open? What clues can you get from the picture?

Next, discuss the story's ending and help children connect it to their own experiences. Ask:

✳ Why did Harriet's mother lose her temper? Was she sorry afterward? How did Harriet and her mother solve the problem?

✳ Have you ever had a bad day like the one Harriet and her mother had in the story? How did it feel?

Use your discussion to emphasize that everyone makes mistakes—children and parents, too! It's okay to have bad feelings sometimes. Parents and children may sometimes feel angry or sad, but they still love each other very much.

Feelings Faces (Social Studies, Language Arts, and Art)

In this collaborative book, children practice "making faces" to express a variety of emotions.

1. Begin a discussion about facial expressions with children. Ask: *How does your face look when you are happy? Sad? Angry? What other feelings do you have faces for?* On the board or chart paper, brainstorm a list of feelings words. In addition to words like *happy* and *sad*, suggest vocabulary words such as *calm, frustrated, disappointed, excited, amazed,* and so on.

2. Make a copy of the page template on page 21 for each child, and read the poem aloud. Invite children to choose a feelings word from the list to fill in the blank, or use a word of their own. Then provide children with crayons, yarn, and collage materials and have them create a self-portrait on the blank face to show the emotion. If possible, give children hand mirrors to guide their illustrations. They can make faces in the mirror and then draw what they see!

3. When children are finished, gather their pages and cut sheets of construction paper for the covers. Give your book a title, such as "Our Many Faces," and bind the book with staples or yarn. Invite children to read the book, identify each emotion, and imitate each face they see.

Moms & Dads Are Special (Language Arts and Art)

Children don't have to wait for Mother's or Father's Day to tell their parents how much they love them! Celebrate the special relationships between parents and children with a surprise card. Provide each child with a sheet of folded construction paper. On the front, have children draw a picture of themselves with their mother, father, or any adult who helps take care of them. They might like to draw a special activity they do with their parent. On the inside, have children write or dictate words to complete the sentence stem *My mom/dad is special because….* Children can write about anything they are thankful for, such as *she plays basketball with me* or *he tucks me in every night.* Have children take their cards home to give to their parents. It's a simple gift that will brighten any busy mom or dad's day!

Word Play

Reread the story, asking children to listen for Harriet's mother's repeated lines: "Harriet, my darling child. Harriet, you'll drive me wild." Draw children's attention to the word *you'll.* What does the apostrophe mean? Explain that this word is a contraction. The apostrophe takes the place of the missing letters. What two words were shortened to make the word *you'll*? (*you will*).

Look through the story for additional contractions, such as *didn't, shouldn't,* and *hadn't.* Can children think of any other contractions? Create a list on chart paper, writing each contraction and inviting children to supply the words that make up each one.

Simon Says... Be Happy! (Movement and Social Studies)

Explore emotions through movement with a game of "Feelings Simon Says." Give children instructions such as *Simon says be happy, Simon says be surprised, Simon says be angry*, and so on. Children can make up their own movements to express each emotion, such as jumping up and down (excited), stomping their feet (mad), and so on. Invite volunteers to take turns being "Simon" and giving their own directions to the group.

Oops! Coupons (Language Arts and Social Skills)

Just like Harriet Harris, everybody makes mistakes! And just as in the story, a warm hug can help to make up for them. Invite children to create coupons to show their love after a goof—or anytime!

1. Begin a discussion about making mistakes. Explain that it's okay to make a mistake—everyone does it! The important thing is to say you're sorry. Discuss the "goofs" Harriet made in the story. Have children ever made mistakes like these?

2. Give each child a copy of the Oops! Coupon on page 21. Invite children to think of a goof Harriet made in the story, such as spilling her glass of juice or dripping paint on the carpet. What might she do to show she's sorry? She might give a hug, a kiss, or a special favor, such as helping to set the table. Have children write or dictate words to fill in their coupons, writing the goof on the first line and the good deed on the last two lines. Invite them to decorate their coupon with crayons. You can post the coupons on a bulletin board to give children good-deed ideas after they make "goofs" themselves.

3. Keep a supply of Oops! Coupons in the writing center and encourage children to use them whenever they'd like. This is a great way to foster self-esteem, responsibility, and a caring classroom community!

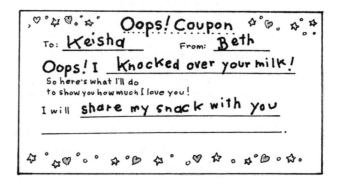

Name

I have many faces—
Here's one for our book.
When I'm feeling

This is how I look!

Oops! Coupon

To _____ From _____

Oops! I _____!

So here's what I'll do,
to show you how much I love you!

I will _____

_____.

Whoever You Are

♦♦

(HARCOURT, 1997)

Concepts and Themes

▲▲▲▲▲▲

☼ world cultures, diversity

☼ alike and different

☼ friendship

☼ self-concept

All over the world, children laugh, cry, play, learn, and love. They wear different clothes, live in different homes, and speak different languages. Their lives may be very different, but inside, they are very much the same—whoever they are. This beautifully illustrated, lyrical book celebrates the diversity—and commonalities—of cultures and children around the globe.

Before Reading

Start a discussion about the ways in which children are alike and different. You might begin by inviting two children to stand next to each other. Ask:

✳ How are these two children alike? How are they different?

Invite the group to discuss traits such as hair color, eye color, favorite activities, brothers and sisters, and so on. Continue inviting different pairs of children to stand up, discussing their differences and commonalities. Can children think of one thing they all have in common? They all go to school together!

Next, show children the cover of the book and invite them to look at the illustration. Ask:

✳ How are the children on the cover alike? What makes each child different?

✳ Where do you think each child lives? How might these places be different from where you live?

After Reading

Page through the book once again slowly, inviting children to take a close look at each illustration. Ask questions such as:

✳ What are these people wearing? What are they doing? In what kind of place do they live?

✳ How are the people in this picture like you? How are they different from you?

Encourage children to make connections with each illustration in the story. Then help them connect with the concepts by asking:

✳ Have you ever made friends with someone who was from a different place? What was this person like? What kinds of things did you do together?

✳ How could you make friends with someone who speaks a different language?

✳ What do you think the author meant by "smiles are the same, and hearts are just the same"? Do you think children have the same kinds of feelings no matter where they are from? Why or why not?

Handy Hello Wreath (Social Studies, Language Arts, and Art)

Children can create a "handy" door decoration to welcome the world into their classroom.

1. Cut a large circle from tagboard or scrap cardboard and then cut out the middle to create a wreath shape.

2. Provide children with sheets of light-colored construction paper. Children can work in pairs to trace one another's hands on the paper. Help each child cut out his or her handprint.

3. Next, invite children to tell how they say "hello." Do children know the word for *hello* in any languages other than English? Invite any children who speak different languages at home to share their greetings. You can also look in library books or on the Internet for foreign-language greetings. Create a list of greetings on chart paper, labeling each with the name of the language (see the chart below to get started). Help children read and pronounce each greeting.

4. Then invite each child to choose a greeting from your list and write it on his or her handprint. Glue the handprints to the cardboard wreath (making sure each greeting is visible). You can hang the finished wreath on your classroom door to wave "hello" to the world!

"Hello" Around the World

Language	Greeting	Pronunciation
Chinese	*Ni hao*	nee-HOW
French	*Bonjour*	bohn-ZHOOR
German	*Guten tag*	GOOT-en-takh
Hawaiian	*Aloha*	ah-LO-ha
Hebrew	*Shalom*	sha-LOHM
Hindi	*Namaste*	nah-mah-STAY
Italian	*Buongiorno*	bwohn-JOR-no
Japanese	*Konnichiwa*	kohn-NEE-chee-wah
Spanish	*Hola*	OH-la
Swahili	*Jambo*	JAM-bo

Word Play

Read aloud the following phrases from the book: *Their schools may be different from yours* and *Their smiles are like yours.* Point out the words in each sentence that show a comparison (*different from, like*). Page through the book again, helping children find each comparative phrase. Ask: *In this story, what is alike and what is different?* Then help children make up their own comparisons by writing the following incomplete sentences on the board:

_____ *is different from* _____.
_____ *is like* _____.

Invite children to make observations and supply their own words and phrases to complete each sentence, for instance: *My shirt is different from Morgan's shirt* or *My lunchbox is like Kyra's lunchbox.* Invite children to tell how each pair of items is alike or different. (For more practice with comparisons, see "Same and Different" on page 25.)

A Heart Like Mine (Math, Language Arts, and Social Skills)

In the story, children learned that "hearts are just the same" all over the world. You can use this matching activity to foster children's friendships right in the classroom.

1. In advance, cut heart shapes from red construction paper (one for each child). Create matching pairs of hearts by writing a number sentence on each one, making sure that each heart has a matching heart with the same answer. For instance, you might write *2 + 2* on one heart and *5 – 1* on its match. Place all the hearts in a paper bag.

2. As children arrive at school, invite each child to pick a heart from the bag without peeking. Have children bring their hearts to circle time and explain that children with matching hearts will be special friends for the day. Then invite children to read their hearts and find their match!

3. Invite the pairs to do activities together throughout the day, such as sharing a puzzle, creating a painting, or sitting together at snack time. At the end of the day, let children share their experiences and tell what it was like to spend the day with a special friend.

4. You can repeat this activity daily or weekly, reinforcing a different skill each time. For instance, you might create alphabet hearts by writing an uppercase and lowercase letter on matching pairs, or create pattern hearts by drawing matching designs.

Variation: To encourage specific friendships in the classroom, you can place hearts in children's cubbies rather than having them choose hearts at random. Before children arrive at school, place matching pairs of hearts in the cubbies of children who don't often spend time together. This is a wonderful way to help children reach out and foster a sense of classroom community.

It's a Small World After All (Social Studies, Language Arts, and Technology)

There's no better way to learn about different cultures than to reach out and communicate with the source! Today's technology has, in a sense, made the world a much smaller (and more accessible) place. So why not let children find out all about their global counterparts firsthand?

There is a wide variety of international pen-pal organizations specifically designed for electronic classroom communication. Even if you don't have access to a computer in your classroom, you can make friends around the world by exchanging good old-fashioned "snail mail." Here are a few Web sites to help get you started.

◎ **Class Connect E-pals:** www.gigglepotz.com/cc.htm At this site, you can register your class and find another classroom to exchange messages with. Although the registration process is done online, you can choose to communicate with letters once you've found a partner class.

◎ **The Busy Teacher's Café Pen Pal Exchange:** www.busyteacherscafe.com/penpals.htm This service is designed for early childhood and elementary classrooms. You can post an ad on the page for your grade, describing your class and the kind of class you'd like to meet.

◎ **Kids' Space Connection:** www.ks-connection.org/home.cfm Especially designed for classrooms and for children under age 13, you can browse this site as a guest or join to post your own ad. Click on the "Penpal Box" link for correspondence opportunities, or the "Project Collaboration" link to explore collaborative curriculum projects.

Same and Different (Math, Language Arts, and Social Studies)

Help children discover how they are alike and different with this fun hands-on activity.

1. To begin, provide each child with about five index cards. Have children write their name on one card. Then invite them to write one fact about themselves on each of the remaining cards. Facts might include information about families (*I have a brother*), pets (*I have a cat*), likes (*I like to rollerblade*) and dislikes (*I don't like cauliflower*). When children are finished, have them keep their name card and place all their fact cards in a bag or basket.

2. Next, set out two hula hoops or yarn circles on the floor, overlapping the circles to create a Venn diagram. Invite two children up to the diagram and have each child place his or her name card over a circle. Then pick a fact card out of the bag and read it aloud. If the fact applies to one child, it goes in his or her circle. If it applies to both, it goes in the center section. If it applies to neither child, the card is placed outside the diagram.

3. Continue until children have sorted all the cards. Then invite them to look at the diagram and tell how they are alike and different. Place the cards back in the bag and invite a new pair to try the activity.

A Universal Language (Movement and Social Skills)

No matter what language you speak, a smile is universal! Body language can be a great communications tool because almost everyone speaks it, all over the world. Work with children to think of gestures that mean the same thing in every language. For instance, a wave of the hand means *hello*; tapping a chair means *have a seat*; a finger on the lips means *please be quiet*; and so on. Invite children to play a guessing game by having one child make a gesture as the group guesses its meaning. Children may be surprised by just how much they can say without using a single word!

Guess Who? Lift-the-Flap Photo Album

(Social Studies and Language Arts)

With the reproducible on page 27 you can create a class photo album that helps children learn just who they are, inside and out!

1. In advance, ask families to send in a favorite photo of their child (or take photographs of children with your own camera).

2. Make one copy of the page for each child and invite children to fill in the clues about themselves. They can write or dictate descriptive words about their hair and eyes (such as *blue, brown, curly,* or *straight*). Then have them fill in their favorite food, activity or game, and initials.

3. When children are finished, help them cut on the dashed lines around the picture frame to create a flap. Then provide them with sheets of plain construction paper and have them glue the activity sheet on top (being sure not to glue down the flap).

4. Next, have children fold back the flap and glue their photo to the construction paper underneath. (Alternatively, children can draw a self-portrait under the flap and label it with their name.)

5. Collect children's finished pages and bind them together with a hole punch and yarn or O-rings to make your photo album. Invite children to read the clues, guess which child they tell about, and then lift the flap to check their guess. As they explore the book, encourage children to tell how they are similar to and different from each of their classmates.

I am special, so are you.
We're alike, but different, too.
Read the clues and then guess who!

My hair is _____ .

My eyes are _____ .

My favorite food is _____ .

My favorite activity is _____ .

My initials are _____ .

SHOES FROM GRANDPA
by MEM FOX · Illustrated by PATRICIA MULLINS

Shoes From Grandpa

(ORCHARD, 1990)

Concepts and Themes

▲ ▲ ▲ ▲ ▲ ▲

☼ shoes

☼ clothing

☼ family members

☼ gifts

When Grandpa offers to buy a new pair of shoes for Jessie, each member of her family wants to get in on the act. She gets socks from her father, a skirt from her mother, and a coat from her grandmother. The cumulative story builds until Jessie is elaborately clothed from head to toe, and she finally asks for the one thing she needs—a simple, comfortable pair of jeans!

Before Reading

Introduce the topic by inviting children to describe the clothes they're wearing today. Then ask:

✳ Do you have a favorite piece of clothing to wear, such as a special hat, a lucky shirt, or a colorful scarf? What does it look like? Why do you like it?

✳ Do you wear different types of clothing to do different activities? For instance, what would you wear to play outside? What would you wear to dress up for a party?

✳ How do you dress for different kinds of weather? Do you have special clothes for when it's raining or snowing outside? What do you wear on a hot day?

Show children the cover of the book and read the title aloud. Ask:

✳ Have you ever gotten shoes or another item of clothing as a gift?

After Reading

Invite children to retell the story and share their reactions by asking:

✳ Why did Jessie need new shoes? When was the last time you had to get new shoes? What kind did you get?

✳ What other items of clothing did Jessie get from her relatives? Which would you like to wear? What was your favorite?

✳ Do you think Jessie liked the gifts she got? Why or why not?

✳ What gift did Jessie ask for at the end of the story? Why do you think she wanted a pair of jeans?

✳ Which do you like better—dressing up in fancy clothes, or wearing jeans and a T-shirt? Why?

Shoe Stew (Math)

You can use children's shoes in a variety of ways to build matching, sorting, and classification skills. Here are a few fun ideas to try.

◎ Go on a shoe hunt! Have each child remove one shoe. Then have children cover their eyes as you hide the shoes in various spots around the room. When all the shoes are hidden, let children open their eyes and go shoe-hunting. Explain that each child must find a shoe that does *not* belong to him or her. When all the shoes have been collected, gather children in a circle. Challenge children to return each shoe to the correct owner by matching it up with the one he or she is still wearing!

◎ Buckles, straps, laces, and Velcro—these are just some of the many features of footwear! Gather children in a circle and have each child remove one shoe. Place all the shoes in a pile and challenge the group to sort them into categories by feature (laces/no laces), design (stripes/no stripes), or even sole texture (bumpy/smooth).

◎ Have each child remove one shoe, and use the shoes to create a graph. Decide on categories for your graph, such as *sneakers, sandals,* and *boots.* Write each shoe type on an index card and place the cards in a row on the floor. Then let children line up the appropriate shoes in each column. Together, discuss the results. How many children are wearing sneakers today? Are more children wearing sandals or boots?

I'm Packing My Suitcase (Language Arts)

Reinforce language and memory skills with a round-robin word game.

1. Seat children in a circle. Start the game by saying: *I'm packing my suitcase, and I'm bringing a shirt.* The child to your left continues the chain by repeating your item and adding a new one, for instance: *I'm packing my suitcase, and I'm bringing a shirt and a sweater.* Continue around the circle, having each child repeat the list and add a new item. How long can children go without forgetting any items? If the chain breaks, just start a new "suitcase" and play again.

2. For a challenging variation, have each player in the circle "pack" one item. The trick is that it must begin with the last letter of the previous item! For instance, if the first child packs shoes, the next child might pack a sweater; the next might pack a ring; the next might pack galoshes; and so on.

Word Play

Revisit the story, inviting children to look for clothing names. Words they might find include *shoes, socks, skirt, blouse, coat, scarf, hat, mittens, sweater,* and *jeans.* Write the words on chart paper and invite children to suggest additional words for the list, such as *shirt, dress, jacket,* and so on.

For a fun extension, hang a clothesline at children's eye level and attach clothespins. Write each clothing word on an index card and challenge children to hang up the "laundry" in alphabetical order!

Community Clothes Drive (Social Studies)

Clothing can make a wonderful gift, especially for someone who really needs it. Invite children to help those who are less fortunate by organizing a community clothes drive. Children can make flyers and posters requesting donations for warm winter coats, gently used shoes, or whatever items best fit the needs of people in your area. Hang the posters around your school building or neighborhood, and set out bins in your classroom or school lobby. Be sure to notify family members as well, and encourage them to donate any outgrown items. When you're ready to make your donation, contact a charitable organization. They will be sure to put your gifts to good use, and children will be proud to know that they made a difference in their community!

Clothes for All Seasons (Science)

It's important to know how to dress for the weather! Here's a fun way to help children sort their "wardrobe" by season.

1. On four large sheets of chart or craft paper, create a "clothes tree" for each season. Draw a simple outline of a tree with branches, and let children help decorate one tree each for winter, spring, summer, and fall. For instance, they might draw snow and icicles on the winter tree (or leave them bare), green leaves on the spring tree, flowers on the summer tree, and red and yellow leaves on the fall tree. Label each tree poster with the name of the season.

2. Provide children with old magazines and catalogues and invite them to cut out pictures of a wide variety of clothing items. Help children find pictures of clothing for all kinds of weather, such as snowsuits, swimsuits, heavy and light jackets, scarves, and so on. Place all the pictures together in a basket.

3. Now invite children to sort their wardrobe! Have children take turns choosing an item from the basket and telling in which season they might wear it. Encourage children to explain their reasoning. They can "hang" their clothing on the appropriate tree with glue (for a permanent display) or removable adhesive (for an ongoing sorting activity).

Winter

Summer

Singles and Pairs (Math)

Post a clothing "problem of the day" to reinforce counting and multiplication skills. You can write the problem on a sentence strip and encourage children to draw pictures to solve it. Here are a few sample problems to get you started.

◎ *Five children wore mittens to school. How many mittens all together?*

◎ *If each child in school today wore a hat, how many hats would there be?*

◎ *Four children went to the shoe store. Each child bought a pair. How many shoes did they buy?*

Lost and Found (Language Arts and Art)

Mittens, scarves, hats, and socks—what child hasn't lost one? You can use the activity sheet on page 32 to create a "Lost and Found" bin that helps children practice descriptive language skills.

1. Make one copy of the activity sheet for each child and have children cut out the clothing cards. Provide children with crayons and markers, and invite them to choose one article of clothing to decorate. You might also provide collage materials such as cotton balls, ribbon, rickrack, and so on.

2. When children have decorated their item, invite them to create a "Lost" poster for it. They can write the name of the item on the first line and then write a description including colors, patterns, and textures. Then have children glue their descriptions to the top half of a sheet of construction paper. (Children can decorate more items of clothing and create additional posters if they wish.)

3. When children are finished, collect all the clothing cards that children have colored, attach a piece of removable adhesive to the back of each one, and place them in a shoebox to create a "Lost and Found" bin. Display the posters on the walls of the classroom.

4. Now it's time to return the clothes to their owners! Invite children to choose an item from the bin and then read the posters on display. When they find the description that matches, they can attach the clothing to the poster. When each item has been matched, place all the clothing cards back in the bin and play again.

Additional Resources

Animals Should Definitely *Not* Wear Clothing
by Judi Barrett
(Atheneum, 1970)

Simple text and hilarious illustrations show children why animals' clothing is perfect just as it is!

The Jacket I Wear in the Snow
by Shirley Neitzel
(Greenwillow, 1989)

In another cumulative sartorial story, a little girl describes each item of clothing she puts on to brave the great outdoors. Repetition and simple rebus-style pictures make this a great read-along!

New Shoes for Silvia
by Johanna Hurwitz
(William Morrow, 1993)

When Tia Rosita sends Silvia a beautiful pair of bright red shoes, she is thrilled—until she discovers that they are too big! Children will identify with Silvia as she patiently waits to grow.

New Shoes, Red Shoes
by Susan Rollings
(Orchard, 2000)

In rhyming text, a little girl describes her exciting trip to the shoe store and all the fancy footwear she sees.

Lost!

One _____

Description:

_____

_____

_____

Found!

Found!

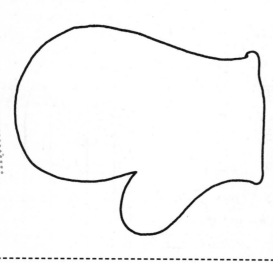

Found!

Found!

Teaching With Favorite Mem Fox Books   Scholastic Teaching Resources

The Magic Hat

(HARCOURT, 2002)

This whimsical story follows a magic hat as it blows around town. As the wind tosses the hat this way and that, it lands on a different person's head each time—with some very surprising results! Children will be delighted as they see each townsperson transformed into a different animal. But never fear—the owner of the hat has a solution, and a surprising identity of his own!

Concepts and Themes

▲▲▲▲▲▲

☼ hats

☼ magic, fantasy

☼ animals

Before Reading

Introduce the topic by inviting children to tell what they know about hats. Ask:

✳ Do you ever wear hats? When do you wear them?

✳ What are some reasons people wear different kinds of hats? For instance, what kind of hat do you wear to keep warm? What kind of hat would you wear at a birthday party?

✳ What kinds of hats do people wear for work? For instance, what does a firefighter's hat look like? How about a police officer's hat? A baseball player's hat?

Show children the cover of the book and read the title aloud. Invite children to make predictions about the story by asking:

✳ What could you do with a magic hat? What magical things do you think might happen in this story?

After Reading

Invite children to retell the story and make connections by asking:

✳ What happened each time the magic hat landed on someone's head? What sorts of animals did the people become?

✳ If the magic hat landed on your head, what animal would you like to turn into? Why? Do you think it would be fun to be that animal? What sorts of things would you do?

✳ In the story, how did the animals turn back into people? Do you think they were glad to be themselves again?

✳ What happened when the wizard put the hat on his own head? Did this surprise you? Why or why not?

✳ If you could be a wizard for a day, what kinds of magic tricks would you do?

Word Play

Revisit the story with children, inviting them to find the words in bold type that name animals: *toad, baboon, bear, kangaroo,* and *giraffe*. Write these words on chart paper and invite children to add more animal names to the list. For a challenge, help children come up with rhymes for their animal words and create a new verse for the story, for example: *It spun through the air for over a mile, and sat on the head of a big crocodile!*

Magic Hat Charades (Movement and Dramatic Play)

Invite children to try on their own magic hat and see what they can become!

1. In advance, collect a variety of inexpensive hats, or use hats children have made themselves (see *Milliner's Magic*, next page). Write animal names on sticky notes and draw a simple picture of each. You might choose to use some of the animals from the story (toad, bear, giraffe) and add a few of your own (dog, horse, snake). Attach one sticky note to the inside of each hat.

2. Place all the hats in a central area, insides down so that the animal labels are hidden. Then invite a volunteer to choose a "magic hat" she or he would like to try on. Have the child look inside the hat to see what animal it will make him or her become. Without revealing the name of the animal, the child then puts the hat on his or her head and "transforms" into the animal. Encourage the child to act out the animal's movements as the group calls out their guesses. The first classmate to guess the animal correctly gets to choose the next magic hat.

3. When all the hats have worked their "magic," write new animal labels and play again!

Magic Hat Wheel (Social Studies)

Hats can indeed be magical—with a special hat, a child can become a firefighter, a police officer, or even a chef! Use the learning wheel on page 36 to help children try on all sorts of hats and the jobs they represent.

1. Make one copy of the activity sheet for each child and help children cut out both parts of the wheel. (For a more durable wheel, copy onto card stock.)

2. To prepare the top wheel, provide children with markers and crayons and invite them to color the figure to look like themselves. Children can color the boy. Help children cut on the dashed lines to create a flap.

3. Invite children to color in the hats on the bottom wheel if they wish. When they are finished, have children place the top wheel over the bottom wheel and help them insert a paper fastener through the center.

4. Now let children turn the top wheel to "try on" different hats. Invite them to read the sentence and guess the occupation. Then have children lift the flap to check their guess!

Milliner's Magic (Art)

With a few simple materials and some imagination, children can create a variety of hats to wear at school, at home, or anytime! Here are a few hat crafts to try.

◎ **Sun Bonnet:** Provide children with a large paper grocery bag and help them cut out one side. The bottom of the bag becomes the back of the bonnet. Then fold back the top edge of the bag several times to create the brim. Let children trim their bonnets with doilies, lace, and rickrack. Punch a hole in each side of the bonnet near the bottom and string with ribbon. Tie the ribbons under the chin to wear.

◎ **Bowler:** You will need an eight-inch paper plate and a five-inch paper bowl for each hat. Help children cut out the center of the plate to make the brim. Then slide the plate rim over the bowl and staple or glue together to create the bowler. Children can decorate their hats with paint, markers, and even glue on a few feathers for extra pizzazz. To secure the bowler, you can attach a string of yarn to each side and tie under the chin.

◎ **Flower Crown:** For each crown, cut a slit down the middle of a large paper plate, leaving about an inch at the edges. Cut four more slits, creating eight triangle shapes. Help children bend the triangles up to create the crown's "leaves." Then provide children with colored construction paper or tissue paper and invite them to create flowers. They can glue one flower onto the tip of each leaf. If children wish, they can staple a few colored ribbons to the edge of the crown so that they will hang down the back when worn.

◎ **Wizard's Hat:** Provide each child with a large sheet of construction paper and let them glue on foil stars, glitter, and other collage materials. When dry, roll the sheet into a cone shape and trim the edges to make them even. Attach a string of yarn to each side and tie under the chin to wear.

◆ Additional Resources

Aunt Lucy Went to Buy a Hat
by Alice Low
(HarperCollins, 2004)

There's lots of adventure and laughs in store when absentminded Aunt Lucy misplaces her hat and goes out to buy a new one.

Jennie's Hat
by Ezra Jack Keats
(Penguin, 1966)

When Jennie receives a plain hat as a gift, she is very disappointed—until a flock of birds follows her home, transforming the hat into a magical creation.

Milo's Hat Trick
by Jon Agee
(Hyperion, 2001)

In another tale of hats and magic, a magician sets off to find a rabbit assistant—and meets a helpful bear instead!

Whose Hat?
by Margaret Miller
(William Morrow, 1988)

Full-color photographs portray adults wearing hats for a variety of professions, as well as playful children trying on each one. The question-and-answer format makes this a great interactive read-aloud.

Magic Hat Wheel

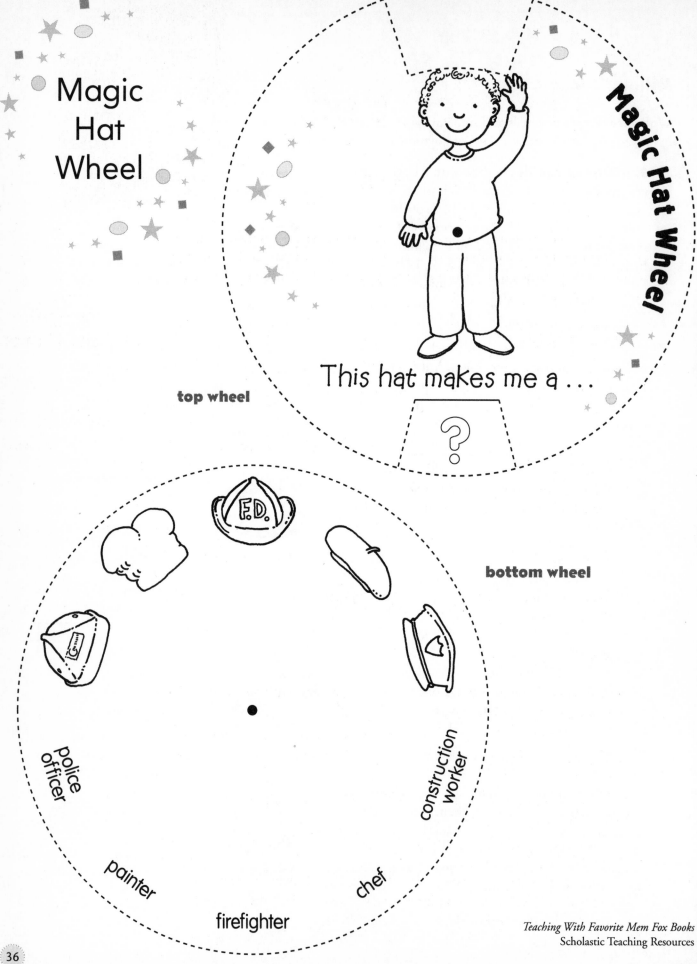

Magic Hat Wheel

top wheel

This hat makes me a . . .

?

bottom wheel

police officer

painter

firefighter

chef

construction worker

Teaching With Favorite Mem Fox Books
Scholastic Teaching Resources

Time for Bed

❖

(HARCOURT, 1993)

Day is over, darkness is falling, and it's time for little ones everywhere to go to bed. In gentle, rhyming verse, each animal parent tucks its baby in for a good night's rest. And as the lullaby draws to a close, it's time for children to go to sleep too. Good night!

Before Reading

Begin a discussion with children about bedtime. Ask:

* How do you know when it's time for bed? What does the sky look like when it's time for you to go to sleep?
* What do you do at bedtime? Put on pajamas? Brush your teeth?
* Does someone tuck you in at bedtime? Who? What does this person say to you? What do you say back?
* What are some things you do to help you fall asleep? Does someone read you a bedtime story? Do you hug a stuffed animal?

Show children the cover of the book and read the title aloud. Ask:

* What animals do you see on the cover? How do you think a sheep might help her baby lamb fall asleep?
* What other animals do you think you might see in the story? How might these animals say good night?

After Reading

Page through the book again, inviting children to name each animal pair. Ask:

* How do these animals say good night? Where do they sleep?
* What other animals sleep at night? Where do you think they go to bed?
* Do you keep any animals at home as pets? What kind? When and where do your pets sleep?

Invite children to connect with the story by telling about their own sleeping habits. Ask:

* What does your bed at home look like? How is it different from where the animals in the story slept?
* Do you think it's important to get a good night's sleep? Why or why not?
* How do you feel in the morning after a good sleep? How might you feel if you did not get enough sleep?

Concepts and Themes

▲▲▲▲▲▲

☼ night

☼ bedtime

☼ animal babies

Pajamas on Parade (Language Arts and Social Skills)

There's nothing quite like a cuddly, cozy pair of pajamas to help children look forward to bedtime. Have a pajama party and parade—right in the classroom!

1. In advance, send a note home to family members announcing your pajama party. Invite them to send their child to school with their favorite sleepwear.

2. Cut a set of cardboard star shapes, punch a hole in the top of each, and string with yarn to make a necklace. Be sure the stars are large enough to write on.

3. On the day of the party, invite children to put on their sleepwear. Seat children in a circle and invite them to describe the pajamas they're wearing. What are the colors, patterns, and textures? Why are these pajamas their favorites?

4. Distribute the star necklaces and help children design an award for each pair of pajamas. Encourage them to use descriptive words and phrases for the awards, such as *most colorful, fuzziest, most interesting pattern*, and so on. They can write the words on a star and sprinkle with glitter to complete the award.

5. When all the awards have been distributed, invite children to wear their award around their neck and march in a pj parade. You might conclude your pajama party with a cozy "nighttime" snack, such as hot cocoa or milk and cookies. Then sing a lullaby, cozy up, and take a rest!

Adult Animal	Baby Animal
mouse	pup
goose	gosling
cat	kitten
cow	calf
horse	foal
fish	fry
sheep	lamb
bird	chick
butterfly	larva
snake	snakelet
dog	puppy
deer	fawn

Animal Baby Word Wall (Language Arts Arts and Science)

Expand children's science vocabulary with an interactive word wall.

1. To begin, look through the story with children and invite them to name the adult animals they see in the pictures. Write each animal name on the left side of a large index card.

2. Next, ask children if they know what these animals' babies are called. On the right side of each card, write any baby names children already know. Introduce new vocabulary words to fill in the remaining cards (the chart at left lists each animal in the story). You can also help children create additional cards for other animals, such as duck/duckling, pig/piglet, goat/kid, and so on.

3. When the cards are complete, cut each card in half in a zigzag pattern, separating the two words into puzzle pieces. Mix up all the pieces and attach them to a children's eye-level bulletin board. Then challenge children to reunite each animal parent with its baby!

Make a Stargazer (Science and Art)

As children learned in the story, bedtime means "the stars on high are shining bright." Invite children to recreate the night sky with their very own stargazers.

1. Provide each child with a cardboard tube (such as a paper-towel tube). Invite children to paint their tubes black. They can also attach foil stars or glitter to decorate the outside of the tube.

2. Next, provide each child with a square of black construction paper large enough to fit over the end of the tube. Help children place the paper on the end, fold the edges down, and secure tightly with a rubber band or tape.

3. Provide children with sharpened pencils or opened paper clips and let them punch small holes in the paper to create a pattern of "stars." For more advanced science learning, you can show children pictures of simple constellations (see below) and help them punch holes in the same pattern.

4. When children are finished, invite them to look through the open end of their stargazer as they point it toward a light source. They will see a lovely piece of night sky!

Variation: You can also create "starlight" in the classroom with a window shade. Find an old window shade in a dark color (or make your own with a large sheet of heavy craft paper, painted black). Let children punch holes in the shade with an opened paper clip or hairpin. They can create free-form patterns, or try to recreate the constellations. Turn off all the lights and hang your "starshade" in a sunny window (darken any remaining windows). As the sun streams in through the holes, you'll enjoy a roomful of starlight! (This is a great effect for rest time.)

Word Play

You can use the rhymes in the story for a mini-lesson on a few common word families. Revisit the story with children, challenging them to look for word pairs that not only rhyme, but also end in the same spelling pattern. A few words they might find include *cat/that*, *sheep/sleep*, *snake/awake*, and *bright/night*.

On a sheet of chart paper, create a column for each word family. Write the appropriate words from the story in each column, using one color for the word beginning and another color for the common ending. Invite children to suggest additional words for each word family list, such as *mat/sat/pat*, *creep/beep/jeep*, *cake/fake/lake*, and *sight/light/fight*.

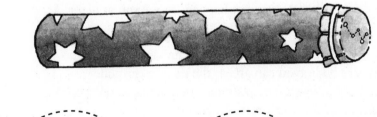

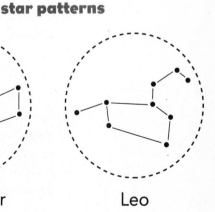

star patterns

Orion   Cassiopeia   Big Dipper   Leo

Ten in the Bed (Math, Music, and Movement)

Invite children to get their "sillies" out as they perform a classic chant that also teaches counting and subtraction skills.

1. Bring children to an open area and set a large sheet or blanket on the ground. Invite ten children to lie down on the "bed" side by side. Then teach the group the following chant:

> There were ten in the bed and the little one said,
> "Roll over! Roll over!"
> So they all rolled over, and one fell out.

2. Invite children to sing the first line of the chant as a group. Have the child on the far right of the sheet sing the lines "Roll over! Roll over!" by himself. Then have the group sing the last line together. Let all children on the sheet roll over once, and have the child on the end roll off the sheet to "fall out." How many are left in the bed? Start a new verse with the number nine.

3. Continue to repeat the chant until only one child is left in the bed and have him or her sing this final line:

> There was one in the bed and the little one said, "Good night!"

4. Repeat the activity, rotating groups until each child has had at least one turn on the "bed."

What Makes Night? (Science)

Here's a fun, kinesthetic way to introduce children to Earth's rotation.

1. Invite children to tell what they know about day and night. Why do they think it is light out during the day and dark at night? Lead children to see that the sun is what lights up the sky during the day. So what happens to the sun at night? Does it move? No—we do!

2. To demonstrate, invite a volunteer to play Earth. Get a large world map and wrap it around the volunteer's body (you can attach the map to the child's clothing with masking tape). Position the map so that the United States is on the child's chest. Help children find your area on the map and mark it with a sticker.

3. Next, invite another volunteer to play the sun and give him or her a flashlight. Dim the classroom lights and have the child playing Earth stand with his or her back to the flashlight beam. Ask children if they think it is day or night in their town. Is any light shining on the sticker? If not, it's nighttime. Then have the child playing Earth slowly turn around (making sure the sun stays in one place). Where is the light shining now? When the child turns to face the flashlight, it's daytime! Explain that as Earth rotates, the sun shines on different parts. When it is daytime in your area, it's nighttime in another, and vice versa.

Bedtime Clock (Math)

When is it time for bed? Children can set their own bedtime clock as a reminder!

1. Make one copy of page 42 for each child (you may choose to copy the sheet onto card stock for durability). Invite children to decorate their clocks with crayons, or sprinkle on silver glitter for a starry effect (remind them to make sure the numbers on the clock remain visible).

2. Help children cut out the clock pattern and hand pieces. Then have them place the hands in the center of the clock so that the dots line up. Insert a paper fastener. Show children how to manipulate the minute and hour hands to set their clocks for different times.

3. If you like, you can let children take their bedtime clocks home. Invite family members to help children set the clock to show their bedtime and use it as a reminder.

4. If you have a regular rest time scheduled into your school day, you might like to have children use their clocks in the classroom. Have children set their clocks to the time your class takes a rest. They can check their bedtime clocks against your classroom clock at various points throughout the day. When the hands match up, it's time for bed!

▲▲▲▲▲▲▲▲▲▲▲▲▲▲▲

Additional
Resources

Animal Lullabies
by Pam Conrad
(HarperCollins, 1997)

This book's poetry and dreamy watercolors explore more bedtime rituals in the animal word.

Asleep in a Heap
by Elizabeth Winthrop
(Holiday House, 1993)

When little Julia delays her bedtime by singing in the bathtub, she lulls her whole family to sleep—proving that even a bath mat can be a cozy bed if it's shared with the ones you love!

Barnyard Lullaby
by Frank Asch
(Simon & Schuster, 1998)

It's bedtime on the farm, and the animals' noises are keeping the farmer awake—but to the chicks, calves, and piglets, they're a beautiful lullaby.

How Do Dinosaurs Say Goodnight?
by Jane Yolen
(Blue Sky, 2000)

"How does a dinosaur say goodnight when Papa comes in to turn off the light?" Children will delight in seeing their sleepy dinosaur counterparts prepare for (and postpone) lights-out.

▼▼▼▼▼▼▼▼▼▼▼▼▼▼▼

Time for Bed

Sleepy Bears

❖❖

(HARCOURT, 1999)

The days are growing darker and colder, and it's time for the bears to take their long winter's nap. So Mother Bear calls all her children into the cave—but how does a bear put her babies to sleep? With a bedtime story, of course! As Mother Bear weaves a delightful dream for each baby bear, they all fall fast asleep until spring.

Before Reading

Invite children to tell what they know about bears. Ask:

✳ What do bears look like? How do they move? Where do bears live?

✳ What do bears do in the wintertime? What does it mean to *hibernate*?

After giving children time to share their ideas, discuss how different animals adapt to winter. Explain that while some animals remain active in cold weather, others are only active in the warmer seasons. When the weather gets cold, these animals let their bodies take a rest. The rest is something like a long sleep. (You might also choose to explain the difference between hibernation and dormancy: Dormant animals' bodies slow down for a lighter sleep, while hibernating animals go into a very deep sleep. Animals such as black bears and raccoons are dormant during winter, while woodchucks and some types of bats hibernate.)

Next, show children the cover of the book. Ask:

✳ Why do you think the bears are sleepy? At what time of year do you think this story takes place?

✳ How do you think the mother bear will get her babies to sleep?

After Reading

Invite children to recall the story and connect it to their own experiences. Ask:

✳ What kinds of stories did the mother bear tell her children to help them fall asleep? Do you like to hear a story before you go to sleep? What's your favorite bedtime story?

✳ Why do you think some animals sleep in the wintertime? How might winter be difficult for an animal? Do you think they would have trouble finding food or staying warm?

✳ What do you think it would be like to sleep through the winter? What activities do you do in the wintertime? Would you be sorry to miss them? Why or why not?

Concepts and Themes

▲▲▲▲▲▲

✿ bears

✿ winter, hibernation

✿ bedtime stories, dreams

Word Play

Revisit the story to teach a mini-lesson on superlatives. Draw children's attention to Mother Bear's repeated lines: "'Now who's the sleepiest? Who will be next?'" Write the words *sleepy* and *sleepiest* on the board or chart paper and ask children whether they know what the *-est* ending means. How does this ending change the meaning of the word *sleepy*? (It means the most sleepy.) Invite children to suggest other adjectives and their superlatives, such as *pretty/prettiest, friendly/friendliest, busy/busiest,* and so on. Point out that when the root word ends with *y*, it is changed to an *i* before adding *-est*.

Why Hibernate? (Science)

To illustrate one reason some bears and other animals hibernate or go into dormancy in winter, try this simple experiment.

1. Gather a supply of "bear food" (small berries, such as blueberries, blackberries, or cranberries) and several ice cube trays filled with water.

2. Invite children to drop a berry into each compartment of the tray. Reserve some berries at room temperature.

3. Place the trays in a freezer, or outside on a very cold day. When frozen, pop out the cubes and invite children to examine them. Can they smell the berries through the ice? Can they eat them? Invite children to compare the ice-covered berries to the room-temperature berries. Which would be more difficult to for a bear to smell, find, and eat?

4. Use the experiment to discuss why bears and other hibernating animals eat as much as they can in the autumn to store up energy for their winter sleep.

Biscuit Bears (Cooking)

This yummy snack will satisfy even the "beary" biggest appetite!

1. Provide each child with two uncooked round refrigerator biscuits (available in tubes) and a square of aluminum foil. Have children place one whole biscuit on the foil to create the bear's head.

2. Next, have children tear the second biscuit in half. They can roll one half into a ball and place it in the center of the bear's head to create a nose. Have children divide the other half into two pieces, and then press them on top of the bear's head to form ears.

3. Give each child three raisins and invite children to press them into their biscuits to create two eyes and the tip of the bear's nose. Have them sprinkle their completed biscuits with cinnamon sugar.

4. Place the biscuits on a cookie sheet and bake according to package directions. Let cool and enjoy—with honey, of course!

Snack Time Bears Place Mat

(Math and Following Oral Directions)

Turn snack time into a yummy experience filled with math learning opportunities. With some Teddy Grahams™ graham crackers and the reproducible on page 47, you can teach number concepts, spatial relationships, and more!

1. Make one copy of page 47 for each child. Invite children to color in the scene if they wish. When children are finished, you may want to laminate the place mats for use at the snack table.

2. Purchase a class supply of Teddy Grahams™ (or ask family members to donate). When it's time for snack, set out the place mats and provide each child with a plastic cup of grahams. Encourage children to use their graham bears to act out a story as you tell it aloud. When the story is over, they can eat up their snacks! Following are examples of stories to tell.

   - *Six bears set off on a walk through the woods. They started at the honey jar. One bear followed the path to the mountain and climbed up to the top. Two bears stopped to smell the flowers in the flower patch. The rest of the bears walked all the way to the cave and went inside to sleep.* How many bears are outside the cave? How many more bears are in the cave than on the mountain?

   - *Three baby bears were climbing trees. Winter was coming, so the mother bear walked through the woods to find them. First she looked on the mountain. Then she looked in the flower patch. At last she found her babies and took them into the cave for winter. Then the father bear came to join them.* How many bears all together are in the cave?

Going on a Bear Hunt (Mapping and Dramatic Play)

Here's a fun way to incorporate map skills into a hibernation theme activity.

1. Provide each child with a plush bear (or a bear shape cut from cardboard) and have children label the bear with their name. Then encourage children to find a secret "cave" in the classroom for their bear to hibernate in. Children can hide their bears on bookshelves, behind an easel, and so on.

2. Next, provide children with paper and crayons and encourage them to draw a map of the classroom. Have them mark an *X* on the spot where their bear is hibernating, write their name, and then trade maps.

3. Now let the bear hunt begin! Children can imagine that spring has arrived and it is time to wake up the bears. Have children use the map to find their partner's bear. When they find the bear with the correct name, they can give it a spring wake-up call and bring it out of its cave.

Tip

▲▲▲▲▲▲

To create more challenging stories, you might provide children with two flavors of bear grahams: honey or cinnamon grahams can represent brown bears, and chocolate grahams can represent black bears. Use the colors in your stories, for instance: *Two black bears and five brown bears were in the trees. Four black bears were on the mountain. Are there more black bears or brown bears out today?* For more whimsically colored bear stories, you might even try using gummy candy. You can also do this activity in the math center rather than at snack time—just use plastic counting bears instead of food.

Sleepy Bear Sleepover Journal

(Language Arts and Social Studies)

For a truly fun way to forge a home-school connection, you can "adopt" a class bear and keep a journal about his travels!

1. Purchase a teddy bear for the class, or ask a family to donate one. Introduce the bear to children and explain that they will all be helping to take care of him. After all, a sleepy bear needs a place to sleep—so this one will be having lots of sleepovers! Tell children that the bear will spend one night in each of their homes.

2. Make one copy of page 48 for each child. You might also like to prepare and copy a family letter explaining your project. Tell families that the class bear will help children learn more about each other and their homes. Keeping a journal will also help children develop language and writing skills.

3. On a rotating basis, send each child home with the bear, a journal page, and your family note. Encourage families to involve the bear in whatever activities they normally do at home: He can sit at the dinner table, join in on a game, or listen to a story. Ask families to help their child fill in the journal page describing the bear's night at their home, and have them return it to school along with the bear.

4. When each child has had a sleepover, stack children's pages and cut on the dotted line to make a bear-shaped sleepover journal. Using a cut page as a template, you can create bear-shaped covers from brown construction paper. Punch holes in the pages where indicated and bind with yarn to complete the book. Share the completed journal with children, inviting them to tell about the bear's experiences in each child's home.

NOTE: You can sanitize the teddy bear by running it through a laundry cycle.

HONEY

Teaching With Favorite Mem Fox Books   Scholastic Teaching Resources

Teaching With Favorite Mem Fox Books   *Scholastic Teaching Resources*

My Sleepover at

_____'s

House

Date: _____

What I ate:

_____

Where I slept:

_____

What I did:

_____

_____

_____

Hattie and the Fox

❖❖

(SIMON & SCHUSTER, 1986)

Hattie and the Fox
by Mem Fox
Illustrated by Patricia Mullins

When Hattie the hen sees a mysterious nose poking out of the bushes, she warns all of her animal friends on the farm—but no one seems to listen. As Hattie keeps watch, one body part after another begins to emerge. When the fox appears at last, the animals finally take notice—and the cow comes up with a unique solution.

Concepts and Themes

▲▲▲▲▲▲

☼ farms
☼ farm animals
☼ animal sounds
☼ body parts

Before Reading

Invite children to tell what they know about farm animals. Ask:

✳ What kinds of animals live on a farm?

✳ Why do you think farmers keep these animals? What does each animal do on the farm? What are their jobs?

✳ What kinds of animals do not belong on a farm? Why not? What do you think might happen if an animal such as a fox or a wolf got into a barnyard?

Show children the cover of the book and read the title aloud. Invite children to make predictions by asking:

✳ Do you think a hen and a fox would get along well together?

✳ What kind of expression does Hattie have on the cover? How do you think she is feeling? Why?

✳ What other animals do you think you will see in this story?

After Reading

Encourage children to resequence the story by asking:

✳ What body part did Hattie first see through the bushes? Do you think she knew it belonged to a fox?

✳ What did Hattie's farm friends say when she warned them of the danger? Why didn't they listen?

✳ What part of the fox did Hattie see next? What did she do?

Next, discuss the ending of the story with children. Ask:

✳ How did the cow help the farm animals solve their problem? Did this surprise you? Why or why not?

✳ What lesson did the animals learn at the end of the story? Do you think they will listen to Hattie next time?

✳ Do you think the fox will return to the farm? Why or why not?

Word Play

Revisit the story with children to find the words that name body parts. Words they might find include: *nose, eyes, ears, legs, body,* and *tail.* Write these words on index cards and invite children to suggest additional words, such as *feet, paws, beak, snout, hands, arms, wings,* and so on. You can invite children to sort the cards in a variety of ways. For instance, they can create one pile for parts that belong only to animals and one for parts that belong to both animals and people. Children can also sort their words by parts that come in ones, twos, and fours.

Barnyard Relay (Movement and Language Arts)

Invite children to act out their favorite farm animals with a fun movement activity.

1. Write on slips of paper animal names such as *sheep, cow, goose, pig, horse, hen,* and so on. Place all the slips in a basket.

2. Divide the class into two teams and mark a starting line on the floor with masking tape. Have each team line up behind the starting line, and place the animal basket between them.

3. Now let the relay begin! When you say, *Go!* have the first child on each team reach into the basket, read the animal word, and then move the way that animal would to the end of the room and back. Encourage children to use both movements and sounds to portray their animal. When the child returns, the next player reaches into the basket for a new animal. (Children can discard their animal words after their turn.) Continue the relay until all the animal words have been used. Then write new animals and play again!

Storytelling Pull-Through (Language Arts)

Invite children to retell the story with the pull-through on page 52.

1. Provide each child with a copy of the activity sheet and have children cut out the picture and word strips on the dotted lines. Children can use crayons to color in the bushes and the fox if they wish.

2. Next, help children cut the dotted lines on the bushes to make two slits. Have them insert the picture strip up through the bottom of the page and through the top slit so that the "Pull" tab pokes through. (The remainder of the strip should stay behind the page.) Then have children do the same for the word strip, inserting it through the bottom slit.

3. Now let children tell their stories. By pulling slowly on the picture strip, children will see the fox gradually emerge from the bushes, just like in the book. As each part of the fox appears, invite children to pull on the word strip to create a sentence that matches what they see. They can alternate pulling on each strip until the fox has leaped out from the bushes and the sentence is complete. Invite children to tell their stories aloud to a partner.

4. For a fun extension, you can provide children with blank paper strips to make up a new story. They can draw their own animal on the picture strip and write its body parts on the word strip. Invite children to tell their new story to the group and see if they can guess what's hiding in the bushes!

Cluck-a-Doodle-Do! (Science and Art)

Explore sound vibration and amplification with a hen that really clucks!

1. In advance, collect one 8-ounce plastic drinking cup (preferably yellow) for each child. Use a pencil tip to punch two holes in the bottom of each cup, about a half inch apart.

2. Provide each child with a cup and an approximately 24-inch length of cotton string or cord. Show children how to hold the cup upside down and thread the string up through one hole and down through the other. (The strings should hang down from the cup when it is held upside down; the upside-down cup will form the hen's head.) Help children tie a knot to secure it inside the cup.

3. Then let children decorate their cups to look like hens. They can glue red yarn on the bottom of the cup to make a comb. They can create the hen's face on the side of the cup by gluing on black felt circles or wiggle eyes for eyes and an orange felt triangle for a beak. Finally, give each child a cut piece of sponge (about 1 by 2 inches). Help children tie the sponge to the end of one string.

4. Now it's time to make some noise! Have children dampen their sponges with water. While holding the cup in one hand, have them wrap the sponge around the top of the other string and then slide it down the length of the string. The cup will produce an amplified noise that sounds just like a hen's cluck!

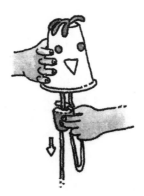

5. Invite children to experiment with different clucking sounds. They can move the sponge in short jerks to create staccato clucks, or slide it down smoothly to create a long squawk. Does the pitch change depending on where children place the sponge? (The pitch becomes lower the farther down the sponge is placed—a longer string produces lower vibrations.) Does the hen cluck as well with a dry sponge? (No—the friction of the water helps produce the vibration that makes the sound.)

Additional Resources

The Chicken Sisters
by Laura Numeroff
(HarperCollins, 1997)

This wacky fable features three eccentric birds who save their neighborhood from a big, bad wolf.

Flossie and the Fox
by Patricia McKissack
(Dutton, 1986)

This story follows Flossie as she travels through the woods to deliver a basket of eggs. On her way, she meets a fox—but this sly heroine proves she can be quite foxy herself!

The Little Red Hen
by Paul Galdone
(Clarion, 1979)

The industrious hen's animal friends learn a lesson about helpfulness in this classic farmyard story.

Rosie's Walk
by Pat Hutchins
(Simon & Schuster, 1968)

In another classic pairing of fox and fowl, Rosie the hen takes a stroll on the farm and unwittingly foils the hungry fox who follows her.

PULL

PULL

a nose, two eyes, two ears, four legs, and a tail!

I can see...

Zoo-Looking

❖❖

(MONDO, 1996)

This simple rhyming story follows Flora and her father as they spend a fun-filled day at the zoo. Flora looks at the penguin, the ostrich, the zebra, the monkey, and more—and each animal friend looks back. The day comes to a perfect close as Flora looks at the most special companion of all—and her father smiles back.

Before Reading

Invite children to share any prior experiences they may have had at the zoo. Ask:

❋ Have you ever been to the zoo? What zoo did you visit? With whom?

❋ What kinds of animals did you see at the zoo? What did each one look like? What were the different animals doing?

❋ Do the animals at the zoo live in different kinds of habitats? What animals did you see in or near the water? What animals did you see in the trees?

❋ Do you have a favorite animal to see at the zoo? Why do you like it?

Show children the cover of the book and read the title together. Ask:

❋ What animal do you see on the cover?

❋ What other animals do you think the girl will see at the zoo?

You might like to write children's predictions on chart paper and revisit the list after reading.

After Reading

Invite children to retell Flora's day at the zoo with questions such as:

❋ Which animal did Flora see first? What did this animal do? What other animals did Flora see on her trip? What did each one look like?

If you created a list of animal predictions before reading, revisit the list and discuss which animals children predicted correctly. Were there any animals in the story that surprised them? Next, invite children to relate to Flora's experiences. Ask:

❋ Have you ever looked at an animal in the zoo and seen it look back at you? What might the animal have been thinking? Do you think the animals at the zoo are curious about the people who visit them?

❋ What senses besides sight do you use at the zoo? What things can you hear, taste, smell, and touch?

Concepts and Themes

▲▲▲▲▲▲

☼ zoos

☼ zoo animals

☼ senses: sight

Word Play

Invite children to revisit the story for a zoo animal word hunt. Animal words children might find include: *giraffe, panther, tiger, snake, penguin, monkey, ostrich, zebra, koala, gorilla, bear, camel, elephant,* and *yak.* Write the words on index cards and invite children to suggest additional animal names. You might have children put the animals in alphabetical order. Challenge them to suggest animals for each missing letter and make your own animal alphabet frieze.

Animal Tracks Accordion Book (Language Arts and Art)

Invite children to create a collaborative rhyming accordion book with the reproducible on page 56.

1. Give each child a copy of the page and have children each choose a zoo animal to draw and write about. They might choose an animal from the story, or choose a favorite animal of their own.

2. Ask children what they think their animal's tracks look like. What shape is the animal's foot? Does it have paws, claws, or webbed feet? Invite children to draw their animal's tracks along the path on the top half of the page. Provide pictures of animal tracks for reference or, if you have toy zoo animals available, children might enjoy dipping the animals in washable paint and then "walking" them across the page.

3. On the bottom half of the page, have children draw a picture of their animal looking out of the frame. Invite them to write their animal's name on both lines. Then have children cut the page in half on the dotted line.

4. When children are finished, collect their work and tape the pages together side by side. Start with an animal track page and follow with the animal's portrait page. Fold the pages back and forth to create an accordion-style book.

5. When complete, children will have their own innovative rhyming zoo book. Invite them to read the first page and guess which animal the tracks will lead to. They can then pull to open the next page, look at the animal, and see it looking right back!

Roaring Good Fruit Snack (Cooking)

This healthy snack is fun for hungry zoo-lookers to make and eat! Set out pineapple rounds, maraschino cherries, raisins, and carrot shavings. Let each child place a pineapple round in the center of a plate for the lion's head and place a cherry in the middle for a nose. They can add two raisins for eyes and arrange the carrot shavings to form a mane. Then give a roar and eat up!

One Elephant (Movement and Math)

This traditional rhyme makes a great movement game and reinforces addition skills. Seat children in a circle and teach them the following rhyme:

> One elephant went out to play
> On a spider's web one day.
> He had such enormous fun
> That he called for another elephant to come.

Once children are familiar with the rhyme, invite one child to stand up and move around the circle like an elephant as the group recites it. Then let that child choose the next "elephant" by tapping a classmate. Have the two elephants join "trunks" and "tails" to make a chain in the following manner: The first child holds one arm forward like a trunk and reaches the other arm back through his or her legs. The child behind grabs the "tail" by reaching forward with his or her "trunk" arm. Start the rhyme again with the number two, and then add one more elephant to the chain. Continue counting up and adding elephants until each child has joined the chain. Then have an elephant parade around the classroom!

Zoo-Guessing Party (Language Arts)

Children can play a zoo animal guessing game while honing oral language skills.

1. In advance, write the name of a zoo animal—*zebra, lion, panda, gorilla,* and so on—on a self-adhesive note for each child. Place one note on each child's back without letting children see their own animal name.

2. Then let the zoo party begin! Invite children to mingle as they ask one another questions to discover their secret animal identities. For instance: *Am I furry? Do I have stripes? Do I climb trees?* The trick is that children can only ask yes-or-no questions. For instance, *Do I eat bananas?* follows the rules, but *What do I eat?* does not. Encourage children to rotate and "interview" at least four other players before making their guess. When each child has guessed his or her secret animal, you can redistribute the labels and play again.

Additional Resources

Brown Bear, Brown Bear, What Do You See?
by Bill Martin, Jr.
(Holt, 1983)

This beloved story features a host of brightly colored animals to look at—and just like the animals in *Zoo-Looking*, they look right back!

Color Zoo
by Lois Ehlert
(HarperCollins, 1989)

With its cutout pages, vivid colors, and striking shapes, this Caldecott Honor book depicts zoo animals in a dazzling and unique way.

Good Night, Gorilla
by Peggy Rathmann
(Putnam, 1994)

Unaware that a mischievous gorilla has taken his keys, a zookeeper wishes all the animals good night and heads for home—with a zooful of animals right behind him!

If I Ran the Zoo
by Dr. Seuss
(Random House, 1950)

In this classic story, young Gerald McGrew tells just how different things would be if he ran the zoo.

I went to the zoo

and I followed this track

Then I looked at the _____

and the _____ **looked back!**

Koala Lou

(HARCOURT, 1989)

"Koala Lou, I DO love you!" So her mother tells her every day. But when Koala Lou's brothers and sisters are born, her mother doesn't have time to say it quite as often. So Lou enters the Bush Olympics with the hope of winning the gum tree climbing event—and her mother's attention. This wonderful story teaches a powerful lesson about unconditional love: Although Koala Lou comes in second in the Olympics, she learns that she will always be first in her mother's heart.

Concepts and Themes

▲ ▲ ▲ ▲ ▲ ▲

☼ Australian animals

☼ sports, Olympics

☼ families, new siblings

Before Reading

Introduce the story by discussing one of its major themes: the arrival of new siblings in a family. Invite children to share their experiences by asking:

✳ Do you have any siblings? Is it fun to have brothers and sisters? What kinds of things do you do together?

✳ What's hard about having siblings? Is it sometimes difficult to share your parents' attention? Why?

✳ Do you have any brothers or sisters who were born after you? How did you feel when you found out there was going to be a new baby in the family? What happened when the baby arrived?

Invite children who do not have siblings to join in the discussion by telling what they think it would be like to have a brother or a sister. Next, show children the cover of the book and read the title. Ask:

✳ Have you ever seen a koala at the zoo? What did it look like?

✳ What adventures do you think Koala Lou will have in this story?

After Reading

Invite children to retell the story and make connections by asking:

✳ How did Koala Lou feel when her brothers and sisters were born?

✳ Why did Koala Lou want to win the gum tree climbing event? How did she feel when she came in second? Have you ever worked hard to win a contest or reach a goal? What happened? How did it make you feel?

✳ Do you think Koala Lou was happy at the end of the story? Why or why not?

Use your discussion to reinforce the idea that "winning" is not always important; it feels good to reach for a goal no matter how things turn out. Be sure to also point out that parents love their children just for being themselves!

Word Play

Look through the book with children for names of Australian animals, such as *koala*, *emu*, *platypus*, and *kookaburra*, and help children find the illustration of each animal. You might do research to find out more about Australian animals and their unusual names, such as the *echidna*, *wombat*, *bandicoot*, and *wallaby*.

The Bush Olympics (Physical Development, Social Studies, Science, and Math)

Children can learn about Australian animals and Olympic traditions by participating in their own Bush Olympic Games. Before you begin, make multiple copies of the medals on page 60. Punch holes in the top, string with yarn or ribbon, and put the medals aside to use after each event.

Lead children through any or all of the following Bush Olympic events, providing information about each animal as you go. Give each child a medal for participating in each event and have children write their "Olympic record" in the space provided. End your Olympics by letting children march in a closing ceremony parade as they proudly wear their medals.

◎ **Koala Climbing Event:** The koala's long, curved claws help make it an excellent climber. Invite children to participate in a gum tree climbing event, just like Koala Lou. If you have a jungle gym in your play area, you can help children time how long it takes them to climb to the top. Otherwise, you can create a masking tape "tree" on the floor for a horizontal climb. Children can crawl from branch to branch until they reach the "highest" one. Invite children to take turns climbing and help them time their results with a stopwatch or a clock with a second hand. Invite children to record their time on a medal.

◎ **Kangaroo Jumping Event:** The red kangaroo can jump as far as 25 feet! But did children know that kangaroos can only jump when their sturdy tails are touching the ground? Mark a starting line on the floor with masking tape and invite children to take turns kangaroo-jumping. Children can start with their bottoms on the floor, knees bent, and hands on the floor behind them. Then have children jump as far as they can by pushing off from their hands and bottoms. Help children measure their jumps with a ruler and write the number of inches on their medal.

◎ **Emu Running Event:** Emus are extremely fast and agile runners—they have been clocked at speeds of more than 30 miles per hour! Set up an "obstacle course" of cones in your outdoor play area and let children take turns running slalom-style through the course. How fast can children finish without knocking over any cones? Time children's results and have them write the number of seconds on their medal.

◎ **Kookaburra Laughing Event:** The kookaburra is an Australian bird that's known for its infectious and remarkably human-sounding laugh. This silly event is sure to tickle children's funny bones! Invite each child to laugh in his or her own special way and then decide together on an award for each laugh (silliest, funniest, loudest, softest, and so on). Write the superlatives on the medals and present one to each child.

Olympic Torch Treats (Cooking)

After your Bush Olympic Games, serve up a special treat to celebrate children's accomplishments. Provide each child with a sugar cone and set out containers of red, orange, and yellow sherbet. Let children scoop the flame-colored sherbet into their "torches" and add red, yellow, and orange sprinkles. Then enjoy the sweet taste of Olympic victory!

Adopt a Koala (Social Studies and Science)

After reading *Koala Lou*, children are bound to fall in love with its adorable marsupial protagonist. Your class can "adopt" a real koala to help save the species and preserve its natural habitat. The Australian Koala Foundation runs the Foster-a-Koala program to protect koalas in wildlife sanctuaries. Three fostering options are available: You can sponsor a joey, an adult, or a mother and its joey. The foundation will send you a photograph of your koala, a certificate with your koala's name, newsletters, and even a holiday greeting card. For more information, you can visit the foundation online at **www.savethekoala.com/fosterindex.html**, or send an e-mail to **akf@savethekoala.com**. You can also write to the foundation at: Australian Koala Foundation, G.P.O. Box 2659, Brisbane, QLD 4001, Australia.

Koala Family Tree (Social Studies)

Koala Lou had lots of brothers and sisters to fill the branches of her gum tree. Invite children to create their own family tree with the reproducible pattern below. Make multiple copies of the pattern (you may choose to reverse the image for some copies, so that children can balance out their trees with branches on each side). Provide children with construction paper and crayons and invite them to draw a simple outline of a tree trunk. Then let children paste one koala branch on their tree to represent each family member. They can color in the koalas (you might assign different colors for male and female family members) and write each person's name on the koala's tummy. Encourage children to place adult family members higher on the tree, and children below. Post children's family trees and invite them to share what makes their family special.

koala branch pattern

Additional Resources

Australian Animals
by Caroline Arnold
(HarperCollins, 2000)

From echidnas to wombats, this book introduces a wide variety of fascinating Australian animals.

I Am a Little Koala
by François Crozat
(Barron's, 1995)

Through bright illustrations and simple information, a little koala introduces itself and its habitat.

A Koala is Not a Bear!
by Bobbie Kalman
(Crabtree, 1997)

Full-color photographs and simple text help children differentiate koalas from bears.

My Grandma Lived in Gooligulch
by Graeme Base
(Harry Abrams, 1988)

Take a journey Down Under with a spirited Grandma who keeps a variety of animals in her menagerie.

Bush Olympic
Medals

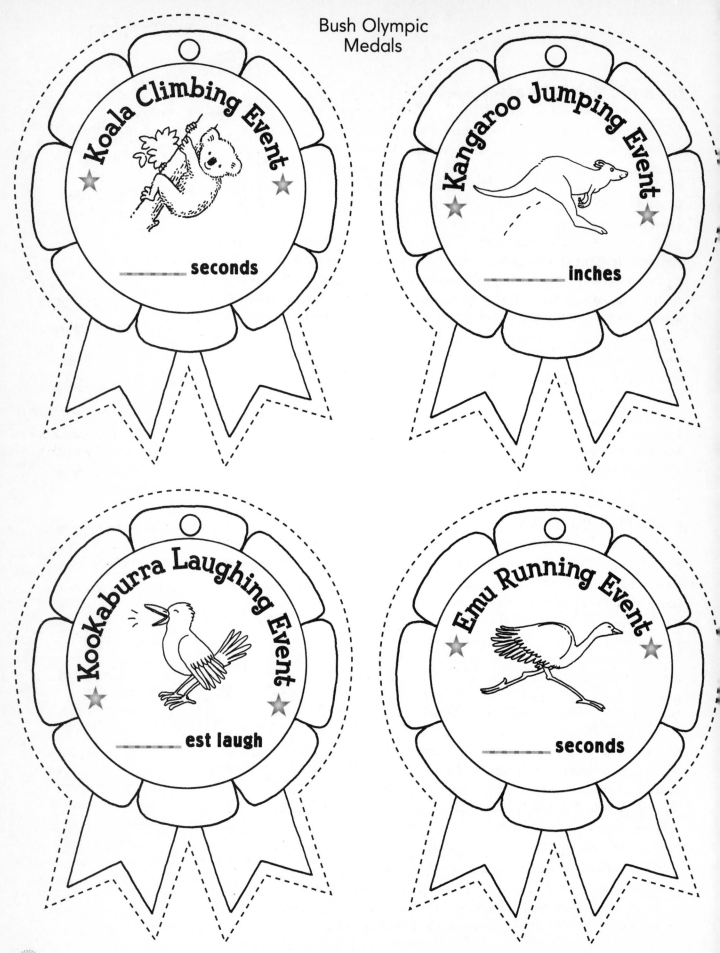

Koala Climbing Event

_____ seconds

Kangaroo Jumping Event

_____ inches

Kookaburra Laughing Event

_____ est laugh

Emu Running Event

_____ seconds

Teaching With Favorite Mem Fox Books   Scholastic Teaching Resources

Possum Magic

❖

(OMNIBUS, 1983)

Grandma Poss makes bush magic, and her best spell of all is making little Hush invisible. The spell is fun at first, but one day Hush decides she would like it undone. Grandma is happy to oblige, if only she can remember the food that will make Hush visible again. Children will enjoy following the two possums on their culinary tour of Australia's cities as they search for the magic cure—and learn about life Down Under along the way!

Before Reading

Show children the cover illustration and read the title aloud. Ask:

✳ Have you ever seen a possum? Where did you see it? What did it look like? What was it doing?

✳ What other animal can you see on the cover? What do koalas and possums have in common?

You might like to point out that koalas and possums are both marsupials (they carry their young in a pouch) and are also both nocturnal animals (they are most active at night). Next, invite children to make predictions about the story. Ask:

✳ What do you think the title means? What kinds of magic might the possums do?

After Reading

Invite children to share their reactions to the story by asking:

✳ What special things could Hush do when she was invisible? Why did Hush want Grandma Poss to undo the magic spell?

✳ Would you like to be invisible? What would be fun about it? What might be a disadvantage?

Next, discuss the setting of the story. Remind children that Mem Fox is from Australia and wanted to write a story about her homeland. Then help children find Australia on a map or globe. Ask:

✳ Is Australia near or far from where we live? How long do you think it would take to get there?

✳ Based on the story, how do you think Australia is different from where we live? Is it a place you would like to visit? Why or why not?

✳ What special Australian foods did the possums eat? What do you think these foods might taste like? Which would you like to try? (For a brief description of each food, see the glossary in the back of the book.)

Concepts and Themes

▲▲▲▲▲▲

☼ possums

☼ magic and fantasy

☼ Australian culture and geography

Mapping Magic (Geography)

Find a large map of Australia and post it at children's eye level. Then revisit the story to find the names of the cities Grandma Poss and Hush visited: Adelaide, Melbourne, Sydney, Brisbane, Darwin, Perth, and Hobart. Help children find each place on the map and mark it with a sticker. You can use yarn to trace the possums' journey by attaching it to the map with pushpins.

Possum's Postcards

(Social Studies, Language Arts, and Art)

Grandma Poss and Hush visited many exciting places on their trip around Australia. Invite children to retell and extend the story by sending a postcard about an Australian adventure.

1. Give each child a copy of the postcard reproducible on page 63. Help children cut out the card on the dotted line, fold the sheet in half on the solid line, and paste it together to make a postcard.

2. Next, invite each child to choose a city from the story to "visit" and send a postcard from. Children can retell that part of the story by writing a message on the back of the card from Hush to one of her animal friends. Encourage children to tell what Hush did in that city and what food she ate. On the front of the card, children can write the name of the city on the line and draw a picture illustrating the scene.

3. You can display children's completed postcards around the room, or invite them to "send" their cards by placing them in their classmates' cubbies.

Tasmanian Treats (Cooking)

Invite children to try the treat that undid Grandma Poss's magic spell! Lamingtons are a traditional Australian food, served at many gatherings and celebrations. You can approximate this yummy treat without using an oven. You'll need a plain sponge cake (cut into squares), a tub of chocolate cake frosting, a bottle of chocolate syrup, and a bag of shredded coconut.

Thin the cake frosting by mixing it with some chocolate syrup. Help children stir the mixture thoroughly until the icing has a slightly thinned consistency for dipping. Next, have children dip the cake squares in the icing and then roll them in the shredded coconut to cover. Let the cakes rest on waxed paper for a few minutes to set. Be sure to sing a version of "Here We Go Round the Lamington Plate," just like Hush and Grandma Poss, as you wait!

Possum's Postcard

Dear _____ ,

_____

_____

_____

_____

Your friend, _____

Australia!

_____

Greetings from

Postcard Front

A Mem Fox Celebration: Culminating Activities

Try these activities to wrap up your author study and celebrate children's learning the Aussie way!

Down-Under Decor

Invite children to take a trip Down Under right in the classroom by creating some Aussie-themed decorations. Show children a picture of the Australian flag and invite them to paint their own on craft paper. Children might also like to create illustrations of their favorite Australian animals, such as kangaroos, koalas, and possums. Have them draw their animals on construction paper and cut them out. Use clothespins to attach the animals to a string hung across the room. Children can also create murals illustrating scenes from their favorite stories. On the day of the celebration, invite children to take on the roles of favorite characters and act out story scenes in their festive Australian surroundings!

Sweets From Sydney

Chocolate crackles are a traditional Australian treat, often served at children's parties in the land Down Under. Why not serve up these easy-to-make sweets at your own celebration? To make about 24 crackles, you will need 9 ounces of vegetable shortening, 4 cups of crisped rice, 1 cup of sifted confectioner's sugar, and 3 tablespoons of cocoa. Melt the shortening in a saucepan over low heat (or in a microwave oven).

Then mix the melted shortening, crisped rice, sugar, and cocoa until well combined. Place spoonfuls of the mixture into paper cupcake holders and chill overnight in a refrigerator. Then say "G'day" and enjoy!

Aussie-Speak

No trip to Australia would be complete without learning a little native slang! Children will be delighted to learn that if they lived in Australia, they'd have some *brekkie* (breakfast) before going to school to see their *mates* (friends). If the weather was chilly, they'd put on a *jumper* (sweater), and if it looked like rain they'd bring a *stormstick* (umbrella). At the end of the day, they'd tell the teacher *cheerio* (good-bye) and go home to have some *bikkies* (cookies) for a snack!

Write to Mem

If you have access to the Internet, you can write to the author on her Web site at **www.memfox.net**. Invite children to compose a class letter telling about their favorite stories and characters and sharing what they learned from their author study. On the site's Contents page, you'll find a guest book link that allows you to type in your letter and post your message on the site quickly and easily. You can also read the guest book's archives to see what other Fox fans have to say. Although the author can't possibly answer all of her messages personally, posting a letter is a great way for children to document their study and share their learning experience with readers around the world.